Becoming an nclusive Leader

How To Navigate The 21st Century Global Workforce

SHIRLEY ENGELMEIER

InclusionINC Media
Minneapolis, MN

Published by
InclusionINC Media
126 North 3rd Street, Suite 412
Minneapolis, MN 55401
www.inclusionincmedia.com

ISBN-13: 978-1-4566-2003-5

Printed in the United States of America

Dedication

For Mom and Dad.

I have the good fortune of having my parents still living.
At age 81 and 88, Mary and Larry Engelmeier are still the most
tenacious and smartest people I know. Thanks for everything!

Table of Contents

ACKNOWLEDGEMENTS

An insightful and gifted group of business people assisted me in making this book a reality. I had the privilege of gaining insights from thought leaders who work for global giants in industry. Their business brilliance provides practical considerations and applications for the important work of becoming an inclusive leader. Their experience, expertise and accomplishments are too many to list in this acknowledgement. In alphabetical order, by name, thanks to Rohini Anand of Sodexo, Donald Fan of Walmart, Manny Fernandez of FedEx Office, Sandy Hoffman of Cisco and Jorge Quezada of Kraft. I am honored you have participated. I thank each and every one of you for your tremendous insights and thoughtful contributions.

Within my own team, there has been a talented and business savvy village contributing to this work. Thanks to Lin Grensing-Pophal and Mike Greece, my first team of co-editors, for their guidance on how to position this work so it garners the absolute importance it deserves in an ever-changing business environment. They each understand the importance of leadership for navigating the 21st century global workforce. Thanks to Kevin Hohlstein, the final editor and proofreader; Kevin ran the marathon on this book, living with it nearly every day for the past two months and never giving up with countless changes from all of us involved. Thanks for sticking with it and insisting on the highest standards from all of us.

To Debbie Scheriff, for your steadfast support of me in all my intensity. To Taylor Vernstrom and Kevin Hohlstein, thanks for the fantastic book cover design. To Dr. Maria Hernandez and Dr. Steve Johnson, your contributions to the book and the Inclusive Leader 360 that is resulting from work in this field are awesome. To Phyllis Jefferson, Jacqui Clelland, and Taylor Vernstrom thank you for your insightful, continued contributions to the cutting-edge leadership learning that is resulting from this book. To Ning Lv and Arnold Guo, from our China office, and Yumiko Suzuki from our Japan office, thank you for commitment to this important work.

Personally, I come from a strong-minded and hardworking gene pool. My mom and dad are both farm kids from rural Minnesota. My parents were literally born in Lake Wobegon—home of Garrison Keillor's fabled weekly broadcasts—where all the women are strong, all the men are good-looking and all the children are above average. That's my family! So thanks to my parents who began this spectacular family legacy of four girls (Shirley, Sharon, Susan and Sheila—for real) and a baby brother Larry (my dad's namesake)! As I begin this new year, I realize how blessed I am with all this magnificence of love, intelligence and hard work in one family unit.

Once again to the men in my life, a huge thanks! To my husband, Russ, who puts up with my energy and my absolutely "nothing is impossible" spirit. To my older son, John Michael, my business peer and the most stunning young person I know, and my younger son, Zach—aka "Boy Wonder," who is embarking on his college career in STEM. Thanks for loving me at the depth you do!

INTRODUCTION

On June 21, 2013 in the Huairou District on the outskirts of Beijing, an American CEO, Chip Starnes of Specialty Medical Supplies, was taken hostage by the company's local workers. Perhaps a modern day "shot heard round the world" with regard to the inversion of power in the workplace, this event should serve as a wakeup call for CEOs in companies everywhere.

With the seismic demographic shift in the global workforce and the dramatic increase in empowerment of workers, the "clear and present" call to action is about the urgent need for managers to adapt to a culture of inclusive leadership. As this dramatic incident illustrates, there is danger in failing to do so. Fortunately, for most organizations, that danger will generally be less a hostage situation than an erosion in the social compact between worker and employer.

The body of knowledge around leadership dates back to the Stone Age—when size and strength were the prerequisites for leading. Over the years, the notion of leadership has been analyzed endlessly, most often focusing on the personal traits, behaviors and experiences of those engaged in leadership roles. But effective leadership is inexorably connected to the context and today, the dramatic change underway in the workforce demands a new perspective on how leaders must lead.

For the most part, the evolving best practices and guideposts related to leadership have been "inside out." The focus over the last century has been primarily on the traditional "command and control" culture where managers and their organizations seem comfortable. Historically, titled supervisors called the shots and the minions saluted. If followers responded without too much angst or pushback, this was all the better. Title trumped reason; seniority often dominated ingenuity.

The hierarchical management ecosystem has existed for centuries—feudal empires and a multitude of corporate dynasties have survived, even thrived, on the notion that leaders lead and everyone else follows. But a transformation in the global workplace has caused an urgent requirement for a new way to lead people. A confluence of contextual factors has changed the game. This book is dedicated to providing a roadmap for leaders to manage and thrive in this environment.

CHAPTER 1:
THE NEW WORKPLACE CONTEXT—
THE 21ST CENTURY ORGANIZATION

Quietly but steadily, the workplace has changed. The context within which leaders lead has become profoundly different for a variety of reasons:

- The internet has given everyone a voice, the means and the power to participate.

- Gen Y[1], who are by nature "participative," have entered the workforce en masse and 46% of Gen Y are multicultural.

- The globalization of the workforce and customer base has created the ability for a broader reach responding to diverse needs and multiple voices.

- New technologies have provided new channels and pathways for communicating that take place with or without formal leaders.

Any one of these factors, alone, would be challenging but not revolutionary. It is the confluence of these factors—which Sandy Hoffman, Chief Diversity Office at Cisco, calls "the collision points" that require inclusion—occurring simultaneously that demands a significant shift in how leaders lead today.

Demographic Shifts

This isn't your parent's workplace (although, there's a good chance that your parents, maybe even your grandparents, are still in it). Poised on the edge of retirement just a few short

---

[1] Generation Y also called Millennials are those born between 1981 and 2000.

years ago, The Baby Boomers[2] are now still firmly entrenched as they wait out the economic downturn in the hopes that planned retirements can be as rosy as they had once hoped. Right behind them, and anxious for them to leave, is Generation X[3] and nipping at their heels is Generation Y. Gen Y is truly destined to prompt significant culture change in organizations not only around the country, but around the globe! And, yes, there is still a fourth generation in the workforce (referred to as Traditionalists or Matures)—those born before 1946.[4]

Whether your company is selling to a global market or not, you are part of a global economy. And we are seeing dramatic shifts, both domestically and internationally, resulting in significant workforce and market changes.

If your business is U.S.-centric, your world is already changing significantly. Suppose that you're a company that serves the Chicago metro area. About 33 percent of the Chicago population is black according to the U.S. Census[5]. Let's suppose you're a company that serves the Los Angeles market. About 48 percent of that market is Hispanic[6]. Take a look around. How many Hispanic people do you see? There are four majority-minority states: California, New Mexico, Texas and Hawaii. The District of Columbia is also a majority-minority population. Within the

---

[2] The generation born between 1946 and 1964.

[3] The generation born between 1965 and 1979.

[4] Catalyst. Catalyst Quick Take: Generations in the Workplace in the United States & Canada. New York: Catalyst, 2012.

[5] US Department of Commerce, (2013). Chicago quickfacts from the us census bureau. Retrieved from http://quickfacts.census.gov/qfd/states/17/1714000.html

[6] US Department of Commerce, (2013). Los Angeles County quickfacts from the us census bureau. Retrieved from http://quickfacts.census.gov/qfd/states/06/06037.html

next decade we can expect Nevada, Maryland, Georgia and potentially Florida to join them.[7]

Why does it matter? Follow the money! The Selig Center tells us that in 2012, the Hispanic market in the U.S. represented $1.2 trillion—larger than the GDP of Mexico. And as in most industries, and most cultures, according to Nielsen[8], the Latina segment of this market is driving a vast number of purchasing decisions that are increasingly influencing consumer product development trends. Consider, for instance, how this impact might be felt during the key "back to school" spending season, or how the decisions of this growing population impact the health care industry. Latino families are increasingly making the impact of their spending power felt in the United States.

Media markets and the advertising dollars that fuel their existence are taking note. Univision, an American Spanish language television network, was the number one network in July, 2013! Each of the major networks is scrambling to create a unique channel for Latinos: NBC Latino and Fox Latino are just a couple of outcomes.

Are you prepared to leave even a small percentage of those $1.2 trillion on the table? If not, then you'll need to better understand—really understand—the Hispanic market and the Latinas[9] that drive buying decisions! Defense is the key word,

---

[7] Teixeira, R. (2013, May 8). [Web log message]. Retrieved from http://thinkprogress.org/election/2013/05/08/1978221/when-will-your-state-become-majority-minority/

[8] (2011, June) *Women of Tomorrow: A Study of Women Around the World*. Nielson. Retrieved from http://se.nielsen.com/site/documents/WomenofTomorrowwhitepaperFINAL062611.pdf

[9] Humphreys, Jeffrey M., The Multicultural Economy, The University of Georgia Terry College of Business Selig Center for Economic Growth—retrieved from http://www.nmsdc.org/nmsdc/app/template/contentMgmt,ContentPage.vm/contentid/2168;jsessionid'28FA6D058AA5087460CEDBF6BEB131#.UaC6krXviSo.

since most organizations have not prepared or acted proactively. Despite the fact that the demographic shift in the U.S. has been a long time coming, many major enterprises did not have the foresight to anticipate the impact these shifts would have on their internal and external growth and success.

While 132 companies on the Fortune Global 500 list are headquartered in the U.S., China (at 89) and Japan (at 62) are not far behind.[10]

Those that continue to hold the top spots on the Fortune 500 Global and Fortune 500 lists[11] represent primarily legacy firms (with the exception of Apple). But there is more to the story. Only 67 companies appeared on the list in both 1955 and 2011[12]. Many have fallen off the list, succumbing to the lethal combination of the web 2.0 revolution, financial crises and the never-diminishing effect of Moore's law—the reality that the pace of change is now exponential. Many have also fallen off the face of the earth—iconic firms like Compaq, Woolworth's, and Standard Oil, among others, no longer exist. Why? Because they failed to adapt their culture to the changing landscape, internally and externally. Because they failed to recognize that their past success did not guarantee future success. Regardless of how brilliant their leaders may have been at one point, the turbulent environment in which leaders found themselves meant that they could be knocked from their perch—or off the face of the earth—in mere months.

The demographic shifts in the U.S. and globally present both opportunities and challenges for every organization.

---

[10] *The 500 largest corporations in the world.* (n.d.). Retrieved from http://money.cnn.com/magazines/fortune/global500/index.html

[11] *Fortune 500 2013: Full List.* (n.d.). Retrieved from http://money.cnn.com/magazines/fortune/fortune500/2013/full_list/

[12] Chew, J. (2012, January 6). [Web log message]. Retrieved from http://csinvesting.org/2012/01/06/fortune-500-extinction/

Enterprises that "get it right" will thrive. Those that don't will be challenged to survive. Changes in demographics require changes in organizations and a more evolved cadre of leaders. As Marshall Goldsmith pointed out in his book, *What Got You Here Won't Get You There: How Successful People Become Even More Successful* (Hyperion, 2007), if you're not poised to embrace the significant demographic changes all around us, you're poised to fail.

Then and Now

The demographic evolution that has been taking place in America and elsewhere over the past several years has had an irrevocable impact on the types of leaders needed to move businesses forward successfully. But, there is a significant gap between the types of leaders needed and those currently at the helm of most organizations.

Most recently, the economic climate in the United States has many organizations in survival mode, shifting attention away from initiatives that could capture the voices and reap the innovation of their diverse workforces. As the economy shows signs of improvement, some organizations have come back to the realization that, without engaged employees whose efforts can yield engaged customers, bottom lines won't budge.

So what it will take for a business leader to succeed in the 21st century is vastly different from what worked in the past. For leaders to ensure that businesses compete effectively in an increasingly diverse global economy, leaders must now be focused on business initiatives that will result in more engaged employees and, in turn, more engaged and loyal customers.

Let's look at the significant change in the business landscape that has led us to this point.

THEN: Past Performance Predicted Future Success

In the past, successful companies were brick and mortar enterprises with clear brand identities centered around a specific product or service. They established their prowess and depended on the people, markets and processes who had created their success. "If it's not broke, why fix it?," was the mantra. Unfortunately, the fundamental belief in consumers staying the same or staying loyal, which was the mainstay of corporate behemoths like Kodak, TWA, E.F. Hutton, General Foods and others, proved inaccurate.

NOW: Companies Must Continually Evolve

Today, even the most stalwart companies and their leaders are vulnerable. The Borders and Blockbusters of the world have learned the hard way that they cannot rest on their laurels. Quite the contrary. Innovative companies like Netflix and Salesforce have demonstrated that even the "big guys" can be knocked from their perch. Today's successful business leaders know that they must continually innovate, not only in products and services but also in the texture and dynamics of the workplace. They know that they must be agile and shift course as the winds of consumer demands change. They know that they must have multiple methods of generating input from a wide range of audiences to fuel future innovation. They also now see younger consumers looking at the brand as larger than a product or service—it's about the organization's social impact too.

THEN: It Was About Counting People

Over the last half century, we have seen increasing gains in workplace diversity starting with President Kennedy's signing of Executive Order 10925 in 1961, that included the term "affirmative action." That was more than 50 years ago, and it led to the passage of the Civil Rights Act in 1964.

Meanwhile, organizations that embraced "diversity" seemed to focus on hiring women and people of color as well as event-based training initiatives—a "dip and done" approach. Over time, these good intentions to create a more ethnically and racially diverse workforce began to focus on "representation" along with educating people about differences. This numbers game, in many cases, lacked clear business linkage. Corporate America has been spinning its wheels for decades, attempting to adapt by focusing on the numbers and it hasn't worked because leaders failed to connect these efforts to the organization's business objectives.

NOW: It's About *Including* People

Becoming an inclusive leader is not about counting—it's about including. While many of us have learned that counting people, alone, doesn't work, we've also learned that *including* people does. *Inclusion* is the new business imperative. *Inclusion* is what will lead to real business growth on a global scale.

Inclusive leaders know that their success depends on the input from the broad community. They know that it is critical to ensure that all employees have a voice. Great ideas can emerge from the mailroom as well as the boardroom!

THEN: It Was About Command and Control

In the old business model, leaders told everyone what to do. Period. They set the rules and held people accountable. They had all of the answers—or so they thought. The best workers were those who showed up, did their jobs and went home. After 30 years they received a gold watch for their compliance. It was a top-down world where everybody knew their place and few dared to challenge the status quo. But that was then.

NOW: It's About Engagement

Today's leaders—the good ones, the *inclusive* ones—recognize that their employees represent valuable capital, not because of their "horsepower," but because of their "brain power." Effective leaders know that organizations can benefit by capturing the hearts and minds of their employees by seeking their input, listening and recognizing that it's not just the people at the top who create value. Good ideas come from everywhere! And good ideas drive bottom-line results.

THEN: Seniority Ruled

The world of command and control was generally inhabited by tenured members of the organization: leaders who had earned their stripes through years of work and reached an age of seniority and presumed wisdom. They held positions of authority and were revered (generally) by newcomers to their organizations—the young, inexperienced ranks whose youth put them at a decided disadvantage in terms of the perceived value of their business contributions. But that was then.

NOW: Gen Y Presents Significant Opportunity

In the 21st century, everyone is a knowledge worker—especially Gen Y. Employees aren't valued as much for their years of service as they are for their brains. And, in a competitive global economy, success means capitalizing on the ingenuity of diverse brain power!

Unfortunately, just as the demand for intellectual capital is exploding, employers are faced with an imminent exodus of knowledge. As Baby Boomers leave the workforce, who will be poised to take their place? Gen Y. This cohort represents the vast bulk of highly relevant and employable available knowledge "talent." Ignore them at your peril.

Gen Y comprises more than 27 percent of the American population and nearly 25 percent of the American workforce today. These individuals will comprise more than 75 percent of the global workforce by 2025 and are already having a disproportionate influence on the workplace. Gen Y is different because they have

- significant fluency with technology;

- little confidence that loyalty to a corporate culture will pay off for them, as it did not for their parents;

- greater comfort with different ethnic groups since 46 percent of Gen Y are multicultural;

- limited patience with the status quo, much like Boomers who wanted to change the world; *and*

- <u>a driving need to be included and participate</u>.

Fail to include this cohort and the results could be highly detrimental to your organization. In 2013, a survey conducted by Beyond.com found that more than 60 percent of Millennials are leaving the companies they work for in less than three years[13]. Why? The greatest reason given is "cultural fit." The message to leaders: be inclusive.

THEN: Business Was Local

In days gone by, people did business locally. They shopped at the corner store. They ate at "mom and pop" restaurants. In the 1960s, if you asked 100 people from around the world where cars were made, they'd likely say "the United States." We were a U.S.-centric economy.

As transportation and technology connected the world and made it "smaller," companies began to sell their goods and services to broader markets—often global markets. But back then, what they sold globally looked very much like what they sold locally and it worked at the time. Years ago, American companies like McDonald's created products that catered to American palates and the rest of the world literally ate them up. That was then.

---

[13] McGraw, M. (2013, August 12). *A Mass Exodus of Millennials?*. Retrieved from http://www.hreonline.com/HRE/view/story.jhtml?id=534355895

NOW: Business is Global

Today, while there is certainly still a demand for American culture and products, developing countries want to consume goods and services that reflect their own tastes. The increased ability of domestic companies to give them just that means America's monopoly on the world's consumers is a thing of the past. Global businesses now require leaders who are culturally aware and culturally agile.

Technology, of course, has fueled the global economy. It is no longer necessary for organizations to be physical, brick and mortar entities or to operate within clearly defined geographic boundaries. Companies can be headquartered in relatively small locales yet still operate globally. They can literally do business from anywhere—and so can their customers. Successful organizations in the global economy are those that best understand these customers, in all of their rich diversity.

THEN: Your Employees and Your Customers Looked Like You

Take a look at company photos from days gone by and you're likely to be struck by the sameness of the individuals in these photos. This was, of course, the impetus for an eventual movement towards diversity—the recognition that organizations were hampered by their sameness, by the lack of women and people of color. That led to the numbers game that we called "diversity initiatives"—the focus on attracting more women and people of color. It wasn't a bad approach; it just didn't go far enough or focus on what mattered most—inclusion as a driver for business. But, that was then.

NOW: They Don't Look Like You Anymore!

Today, the best companies are comprised of a wide range of people inside (employees) and outside (customers). America's traditional "majority" is becoming the "minority." The most recent Census Bureau data indicates that, for the first time, the majority of Americans under the age of one are minorities. Today, 35 of the top 50 metros in the U.S. are majority minorities for kids five and under. In eight of these metros, it's greater than 75 percent.[14] They don't look like *you* anymore, because there is no *you*. Instead, there is a rapidly growing amalgam of *we*—a market populated by diverse individuals based on a wide range of characteristics including sex, age, race, ethnicity, religion, and sexual orientation. How do we get our arms around these changing demographics? The key is cultivating inclusive leaders who can take their organizations successfully into the increasingly diverse and volatile 21st century.

Thus, the leadership challenge for businesses today involves the need to ensure that the voices of both employees and customers are valued and heard.

Massive Shifts Require Concerted Effort

These changes are real and not going unnoticed. In *Forbes'*, "The Golden Age of Management Is Now," Steve Denning points to 10 related shifts that are underway:

1. From maximizing shareholder value to profitable customer delight.

2. From sustainable competitive advantage to continuous strategic adaptation.

3. From a preoccupation with efficiency to co-creating value with stakeholders.

4. From unidirectional value chains to multi-directional value networks.

5. From steep hierarchies to shared responsibilities.

6. From control and bureaucracy to disciplined innovation.

---

[14] Berg, N. (2012, May 18). *U.S. Metros Are Ground Zero for Majority-Minority Populations*. Retrieved from http://www.theatlanticcities.com/neighborhoods/2012/05/us-metros-are-ground-zero-majority-minority-populations/2043/

7. From economic value to values that grow the firm.

8. From command to conversation.

9. From managing the machine to stewardship of stakeholders.

10. From episodic improvements to a paradigm shift in management.[15]

So what will it take for organizations to address these massive shifts? Inclusive leadership. No longer can industrial titans lead organizations to success based on their own perspectives, insights or expertise—however stellar they may be. Instead, they must capitalize on the wide array of diverse inputs that exist within and outside their organizations. This is the benefit inclusive leaders bring to the modern workplace.

Voices Clamoring to Be Heard

Where once they might have hung back waiting for an opportunity for their voices to be heard, today's workforce is empowered by the ability to share their thoughts and opinions literally around the world through social media and the internet. They don't just crave participation—they demand it!

So successful leaders must create work environments that accommodate the new participative urge that has been spawned by an ever-present digital audience they enjoy through the new technology that surrounds and defines them. Old leadership models may have worked when workers exchanged views over the water cooler. But with today's community forums, social media and chat rooms, both the workforce and consumers are hyper-predisposed to share their opinions. This strength of voice has empowered

---

[15] Denning, S. (2013, August 5). *The Golden Age Of Management Is Now.* Retrieved from http://www.forbes.com/sites/stevedenning/2013/08/05/the-golden-age-of-management/

employees and customers, creating an expectation that they will be heard.

Social media, by its very definition, is participatory, collaborative, responsive, validating and equitable—everyone has an opinion and everyone with an opinion feels the right to voice it. This dramatic shift in expectations is a culture shock for many leaders who are struggling with learning to adapt without losing the capacity to steer the ship.

As a result, an effective workplace is no longer a bubble where employees wait to be told what to do and how to do it. It's no longer an environment where companies create a product or service "their way" and expect consumers to flock to their storefronts—whether real or virtual. Today's workers—and customers—expect to have a say in what is being asked of them. It's called engagement and there's no turning back. To be successful, business leaders will now have to learn to accommodate the constant demand for participation.

Today the world has changed and is continuing to change. It's big. It's global. It's comprised of highly participative people with different views, perspectives, backgrounds and demographics. It's fueled by technology which drives the pace of change. In this new world, if you're still leading through command and control, you will perish.

This new era demands "inclusive" leadership. This book provides a roadmap for 21st century leaders to adapt business environments to leverage the insights and input of an increasingly diverse global workforce that will lead to high performing organizations and increased business success.

Key Takeaways

- Significant environment shifts—demographics, technology and globalization—are having a dramatic impact on the workplace.

- The old ways of leading no longer work. Inclusive leaders must exhibit new traits and behaviors to drive success.

- Past performance no longer predicts future success; continual innovation is a must and benefits from input from a wide range of perspectives.

- Command and control leadership behaviors from yesteryear will no longer lead to the levels of engagement required for companies to succeed in today's business environment.

- A global economy—regardless of whether your company is a global business—is having profound implications that cannot be overlooked.

- These massive shifts require a concerted, and continued, effort from leaders who are committed to being inclusive.

CHAPTER 2:
THE JOURNEY AND TRAITS
OF THE INCLUSIVE LEADER

So far, we have discussed the global workplace in the midst of a major transformation—"The Era of Inclusion"—in which many companies and organizations are mobilizing the insights and vision of their diverse workforces to create internal and external advantage over competitors.

But there is a major obstacle to success in creating this environment. Many leaders find it difficult to move beyond legacy management practices. They fear losing control to leadership behaviors that nurture current workers' needs for participation. However, those that have made this shift are learning that this participation can lead to increased engagement, loyalty and innovation—all drivers of business success.

Leaders in all types of organizations—from small to large, from not-for-profit to the Fortune 50, from small entrepreneurial start-ups to legacy organizations—have one thing in common: the desire to succeed. If the organization does not excel, individuals cannot excel. Why do organizations today need inclusive leaders? Why do leaders need to be inclusive? To succeed! The business survival of both leaders and organizations is inextricably linked.

The second obstacle is a lack of experience and skills for inclusive leadership. If I am asking for my employees' input, how do I manage those different ideas? What does inclusion look like among so many different employees? Does being inclusive mean I relinquish my authority as a manager?

The burning question often is how today's leaders can invite participation and collaboration without giving up their authority. How will they embrace this new culture and develop new, more empathetic skills for managing in this environment, many of which will be counterintuitive to their learned and long-practiced way of thinking and managing? They will have to learn to listen, ask, include and welcome new ideas, opinions and insights.

The organic metamorphosis of the new digital workforce will have a profound impact now and in the future for managers. **This is the new leadership normal.** The way leadership has traditionally been taught in business schools no longer works. To be successful, leaders must adapt to a new environment where there are no gatekeepers or barriers to stem the onslaught of input and opinions. Ignoring these inputs is counterproductive. Leaders who fail to adapt will lead the short, once noisy, life of the cicada.

The Inclusive Leader

Many leaders today have been operating with 20th century leadership competencies, says Hoffman of Cisco. Becoming an inclusive leader requires competencies for the 21st century, she says.

Legend has it that good leaders are born, not made. The last century suggests that great leaders can also be made, but only if they can adapt to the new situations and contexts in which they find themselves. That will be the formula for success in the new inclusive business setting. An inclusive leader is one who seeks and integrates the voices of key stakeholders to drive business results.

> An inclusive leader is one who seeks and integrates the voices of key stakeholders to drive business results.
> Shirley Engelmeier
> InclusionINC

An important point must be made here. Inclusive leadership is not about white men learning to "get along" with minorities. Inclusive leadership is about everybody in every organization learning to hear, leverage and learn from other voices within and outside their organizations for the benefit of themselves, their department, their products and their organizations. It's about including all voices—old and young, male and female, Latino, Chinese, etc. Inclusion is for everyone. Being an inclusive leader is not about gender, race, ethnicity or sexual orientation. Being an inclusive leader is about succeeding in a dynamic environment by exhibiting specific traits, behaviors and characteristics that will lead to individual and organizational success.

"Leaders of a team can consciously or unconsciously limit the range of ideas among group members," said Frans Johansson in *The Medici Effect: Breakthrough Insights at the Intersection of Ideas, Concepts and Cultures* (HBS Press, 2004). But he adds, "At the intersection we need as many opportunities for random combinations of ideas as possible. A team of diverse people who feel free to exchange and combine their ideas is exactly what can make that happen." That's the role the inclusive leader plays.

So what does it take to be an inclusive leader in the 21st century?

Traits

There are a number of traits that exemplify those leaders who understand the importance of, and have the skills to elicit and nurture the diverse inputs all around them—internally and externally.

Ego Management

Inclusive leaders are self-aware, which leads to effective **ego management**. They have the capacity to direct their egos situationally, recognizing those times when it's best to be center stage and, increasingly, those times when it is best to hang back and gather input. The right to lead no longer resides in the person with role authority or title— it resides in the person who has the best idea at the time for that particular situation. In truth, it resides in the collective knowledge of a group of people with diverse ideas, backgrounds and perspectives, whose collaborative insights create meaning far greater than individual inputs.

Certainly leaders have strong egos; without strong egos they may find it tough to be effective. In fact, there are many elements of strong egos that are critical for leadership. The key is learning to balance and understand ego and the needs of others to drive an effective culture.

In the past, leaders felt that they were required to always be the "smartest person in the room"—the person with all of the answers. Today's effective inclusive leaders, more often than not, are those who recognize that they don't have all of the answers and are willing to hear the voices of others who may.

Open to a Wide Range of Inputs

Strong ego management lays the foundation for another critical trait—the ability to listen openly. The inclusive leader must have not only the capacity, but also the willingness, to seek and listen to varied inputs, recognizing that the wisdom of the crowd most often results in successful outcomes. "Inclusive Leaders" must be at ease with listening and **open to a wide range of inputs**. This means listening no matter where the input is coming from—the front lines, a tenured employee or a new hire, a Gen Y'er or a retired Traditionalist. It means listening to external voices as well—to customers, to communities, to competitors.

"One of the things that I find is most important is to listen," stresses Manny Fernandez, director with FedEx Office. "Often we get caught up in our workday and, instead of leading, we start dictating and giving orders." Fernandez has found it helpful to share plans with his team and listen to their feedback. They may not be in agreement with what you are proposing, but that's okay because it's part of the inclusion process. "When you allow the team to participate in the process, you're going to come up with a better solution" he says. "One of the things I've learned in striving to be inclusive is to ensure that everyone feels like they have a valued voice in the process, and then to have a bias for action." That bias for action, he says, means being "ready to roll" once you get the feedback you've requested. That bias for action and follow up is critical, especially in a world accustomed to the rapid pace of communication fueled by technology.

At Walmart, Donald Fan, senior director, Global Office of Diversity at Wal-Mart Stores, Inc., adds "we're promoting three inclusive behaviors—one is active listening." Active listening involves some very specific behaviors. "So, when we listen to our associates, we've got to stop doing anything else. We need to give this moment to who we are listening to and pay attention." That's a skill that may sound simple but give it a try. You'll see that it's not simple. But it is a powerful way to convey inclusion to employees. In addition, he says, Walmart is working actively to draw out its quieter employees. "A lot of times our quiet associates have a point of view but they may not feel comfortable to speak up and share. As a leader you need to probe, ask questions and mine their point of view. Our 2.1 million associates across the world are our competitive advantage. We don't want to omit one unique perspective or one creative idea."

> Our 2.1 million associates across the world are our competitive advantage. We don't want to omit one unique perspective or one creative idea.
> Donald Fan
> Walmart

Inclusive leaders must listen with a different intent. Yes, they must listen so people will feel heard. But, they must also ensure they are listening to what is below the surface; that they're listening with intent and purposefulness to seek and understand root causes.

Intellectual Curiosity

Perhaps because of this willingness to continually learn from others, inclusive leaders are intellectually curious. **Intellectual curiosity** is the ability to be continually attuned to, and positively impacted by, the conditions, events and circumstances around us. It's a trait that is perhaps best understood when we think of small children—to them, just about every encounter represents something new. They embrace these new encounters, new experiences and new pieces of information with enthusiasm. They've yet to form the filters that later cause some of us to ignore or overlook the inputs around us because we think: "been there, done that."

Not so fast! Inclusive leaders, without exception, exhibit intellectual curiosity. To be inclusive, it's a must.

Inclusive leaders need to be endlessly curious, says Hoffman of Cisco. "Our organization is 70,000 employees who are intelligent people, probably using one-eighth of their mindset and potential." Inclusive leaders, she says, must be able to tap into the rest of this potential. "To glean the most out of employees, a leader knows when to lead and when to follow," she says. These leaders recognize that there is something to be learned from everyone—their strong curiosity drives them to engage with those around them.

Transparency

Openness and directness, perhaps more than any other leadership traits, build trust that is the precursor to engagement in any organization. Workers in this new inclusive environment follow those they trust. As trust erodes, so does "followership." Trust requires **transparency**. Inclusive leadership requires transparency, and takes a different form depending on how inclusive leaders are integrating the perspectives of those around them. Inclusive leaders must be comfortable giving honest feedback and telling the truth. In a world where tweets travel around the globe with the tap of a key, if they're not hearing it from you, they've already heard it from someone else. This is no longer a world where you can share one message with shareholders and another with the workforce—messages must be aligned, and reflect reality, for better or worse.

"Authenticity is important," says Rohini Anand, senior vice president and Chief Diversity Officer at Sodexo. "Trust is absolutely key, as well as role modeling."

Emotional Intelligence

Inclusive leaders have high **emotional intelligence**. This is a concept that originated in 1990 and was brought forward by Peter Salovey and John D. Mayer, and then popularized by Daniel Goleman. Its relevance resonates even more today as leaders face increasingly challenging and ambiguous situations.

There are four elements of emotional intelligence:

(1) perceiving emotions
(2) reasoning with emotions
(3) understanding emotions
(4) managing emotions

Those who are emotionally intelligent recognize their responses, can take time to consider *why* they are responding as they are, and have the self-control to manage them. This adaptability comes up in a number of ways and is particularly relevant when dealing with diverse groups and cultures—truly anyone whose perspectives or opinions differ from your own.

Inclusive leaders, says Fernandez of FedEx Office, must have empathy—they need to be authentic. "When employees see their leaders exemplify these qualities," he says, "they will reach out to you more willingly." To be effective, inclusive leaders need to connect with both customers and team members emotionally. "It's easy to connect with people on a transactional basis—to just go through the drive-thru window and pick up a Happy Meal® and you're done. But, it's quite another thing to try to connect emotionally.

"That emotional connection is what an inclusive leader needs to encourage his or her team to make because that's going to be the enduring and most productive part of the relationship."

Anand of Sodexo agrees. "Emotional intelligence includes having the ability to flex your style and the cross-cultural skills to really motivate and manage people from different cultures and generations. Leadership flexibility and dexterity is, I think, premised largely on emotional intelligence."

Futurecasting

Those who have a high level of emotional intelligence are often naturally curious—they seek inputs that may be different from their own and they are continually learning from these inputs. But, beyond curiosity, inclusive leaders have the business acumen to generate meaning from the various inputs around them—the ability to **futurecast**. In today's technologically enhanced environment, those who have this capacity are often faced with what seems like overwhelming and conflicting data, yet they embrace this onslaught of information and new technologies. Think about the fact that most leaders today are connected 24/7 through computers, tablets and smartphones. They are faced almost daily with new channels of information; the savviest among them learn about and embrace these—from Facebook and Twitter, to YouTube, Instagram and Google+. Inclusive leaders don't dismiss these. Instead, they use them to their advantage—and the advantage of their organizations.

Were music industry executives caught off guard by Napster? Were Blockbuster and Border's executives asleep at the wheel as technology emerged to challenge their business models? What impact will 3-D printing have on manufacturers? What emerging innovations may one day make what you have to offer obsolete? You can't possibly know if you aren't remaining open to what is trending on social media, emerging on the internet as a whole and being brought to you by your research and development team.

Humility

Inclusive leaders value the expertise of others. They recognize when they don't have the answers, which is often more frequently than not. Yielding to the expertise of others means letting go of ego-centric behavior, letting go of legacy beliefs and behaviors, and being open to insights that can lead to improvements and innovation. They must possess **cultural humility**. Too many business leaders are far too insular in their thinking—they take a "not created here" approach feeling that, if they didn't create it, it has little value. This has been true both as companies compete with other companies and, increasingly, as countries compete with other countries.

Humility involves having not only the wisdom to recognize that you are not always expected to have all of the answers but also the ego strength to admit when you don't and to seek insights from others who do. If you're not a young mother, what do you know about being a young mother? Nothing. But what do the young mothers in your workforce know? A lot. If you're selling products and services to young mothers, their voices are going to be powerful. If you've never been to China and don't know anything about China, what do you know about doing business there? Nothing. But what do recent MBA graduates from China living in the U.S. know? A lot. Inclusive leaders would be open to recruiting them and then listening to their perspectives.

Humility is closely tied to ego management and reflects the ability to recognize that we may not have all the answers, rarely have the best answers, and always have something to learn from others. And, when we do, we must be agile to take advantage of opportunities that emerge.

Cultural Agility

In a global economy, inclusive leaders are **culturally agile** and able to interact effectively with people from other cultures both within and outside of the U.S. It's not, as so many companies think, about teaching foreign nationals how to accommodate to U.S. cultural norms. It's about understanding, respecting and accommodating *their* norms. The lack of cultural agility can result in leaders who fail to identify and leverage opportunities and who lack the ability to form meaningful and mutually beneficial relationships.

The significant shift in consumer behavior means that organizations must be increasingly efficient to remain relevant. They must be consumer-driven more than ever in the past. In the past, companies could create a product and, if the product was good—like a Coca-Cola, it would work. Now though, with a growing diversity of consumers whose attitudes, opinions and preferences are changing, companies must be nimble and prepared to make shifts in their products and services to meet these emerging cultural demands.

Having a global mindset is a core competency for inclusive leaders, says Fan of Walmart. "You need to be culturally sensitive and know some of the details around the style of people who have originated from different countries."

Collaboration

In an era of information overload, inclusive leaders must realize that their best ideas can be fueled by input and **collaboration**.

Collaboration can be challenging in organizations that follow the traditional, hierarchical structure where employees work in "silos." When functions are defined in a very narrow way, conflicts can occur, Fan of Walmart notes. "Because of this structure it's very natural for people to just be siloed and to focus on what they are good at and not pay much attention to the other teams around them," he says. Employees can be the experts in their area, but says Fan, "we want them to be collaborative with the other teams, be systemic while looking for a solution, so that every process or system change will have the best outcome."

"We see the organizational shift from hierarchical structure to a more matrix-driven structure," says Fan. "That means you give up the vertical silos and come to a more horizontal and cross-pollinated environment where collaboration is very critical."

Moving from a command and control, hierarchical structure can take time and may create some conflicts, he acknowledges. Those conflicts, though, don't necessarily reflect pushback, he says. "What you see may not be resistance, but the conflict between the old ways and the new." The key for inclusive leaders, he says, "will be in how they advocate, communicate and help people understand what this change brings to the business and what it brings to individual teams."

Collaborative leaders know that they can leverage radically different viewpoints to create better solutions. They recognize that, when it comes to successfully leading organizations and initiatives, 1+1 doesn't equal 2—it equals some far greater number than this fueled by the power of diverse viewpoints. It's taking a little bit of what's right from my idea, a little bit of what's right from your idea, a little bit of what's right from others' ideas and bringing all of these insights together into a far more powerful result.

Accessibility

To capitalize on these inputs, though, inclusive leaders must be **accessible**. They must be available and willing to listen to feedback from employees, customers and other constituents. Importantly, they must convey through their verbal and nonverbal behaviors— and subsequent actions—that they will be open and nonjudgmental about the information they receive, even if that information is critical of the organization or the leader.

That accessibility can come through technology and it can be extended outside the walls of the organization to customers and consumers. Fan shares an example from Walmart, "We created a program called 'On the Shelf' to help us determine what the best products are and what our customers are looking for." Through its website, Walmart invites businesses or anyone that has invented a product to upload a short video that consumers then "vote" for. It's a concept similar to American Idol, he says. "Our customers are going to vote for the best. We'll pick the top ones and then put them on our shelves through the Walmart.com site." It's a way, he says, of not only recognizing but staying on top of the ways that consumers' preferences are continually changing. "This is really about how we're going to change our business model to adapt to our customers' needs and wants." This is an example of being inclusive through open collaboration and accessibility.

Diversity of Thought

Inclusive leaders demonstrate ease with **diversity of thought**, recognizing that innovative ideas stem from different perspectives, not consensus. "Groupthink" is a term that refers to the conformity that grows among groups that are too alike or that have spent too much time together. They reach the point where the desire to minimize conflict diminishes the ability to create innovative solutions based on inputs that are out of the mainstream. Loyalty and conformity to the group keep members of the group from raising issues, sharing different points of view or challenging consensus decisions. Inclusive leaders are adept at drawing out diverse perspectives and value the differences that those who come from different backgrounds—whether based on gender, race, ethnicity, religion, economics, geography, industry, profession or life experience—can bring to a discussion.

Adaptability

Ultimately, inclusive leaders must demonstrate **adaptability**. While change has been and will continue to be part of the shared experience of business leaders, the pace of change has never been more rapid. Inclusive leaders must have the capacity to rapidly assess the conditions and circumstances around them and adapt to change on an ongoing basis.

It's important, says Anand of Sodexo, for inclusive leaders to display a "flexible leadership style to meet the needs of different populations in terms of what motivates them—being able to do that is absolutely critical."

For 21ˢᵗ century inclusive leaders, adaptability is arguably the most critical competency of all.

Context Changes Everything

These are the traits that will be required of inclusive leaders to lead their organizations to success in the 21ˢᵗ century.

Importantly, these traits are not necessarily different than they have ever been on the surface. What's different is that today's inclusive leaders need to delve *beneath the surface* to get much deeper into these behaviors.

Leaders are often very good at quickly assessing the environment to accurately understand financial issues. Where they may err is in trying to transfer that ability over to cultural assessments. As they do that, there may be a tendency to make assessments too quickly and at a surface level. So they may say: "I don't see any overt behaviors or any red flags, so everything must be okay." What they may fail to understand is the importance of digging deeper—of drilling down to really understand the "why" behind behaviors.

> What do inclusive leaders need to do differently? They need to pause, engage in self-reflection and refine the skills they currently have to achieve real outcomes.
> Shirley Engelmeier
> InclusionINC

Inclusive leaders recognize that it is the sum of all of these traits, and their ability to apply them effectively within changing environments, that will lead to real business benefits.

What do inclusive leaders need to do differently? They need to pause, engage in self-reflection and refine the skills they currently have to achieve real outcomes.

Key Takeaways

- Today's organizations need inclusive leaders—without them, individuals in the new workforce cannot succeed and organizations fail.

- To be successful, leaders must adapt to a new environment where there are no barriers to stem the onslaught of input and opinions from multiple sources, internal and external.

- Inclusive leaders exhibit a number of traits that will serve to elicit and nurture the diverse perspectives all around them—then benefit the business.

- It is important for leaders to reflect upon their current skills and opportunities for inclusive behavior based on their own assessment as well as the feedback from employees and customers.

CHAPTER 3:
HOW SUCCESSFUL
INCLUSIVE LEADERS BEHAVE

It all begins with self-awareness. Effective inclusive leaders are acutely aware of their own personal faults and foibles as well as their strengths. Inclusive leaders are knowledgeable about other cultural norms and can observe and integrate those norms as necessary. They are comfortable with flexing their style depending on the situation and the individuals involved. They can work in competitive, collaborative and cooperative ways. They are responsive to all the business changes discussed in Chapter One. Most importantly, inclusive leaders are able to express and connect to the business case for taking new approaches with employees, customers and other stakeholders. Inclusive leaders are not only comfortable with but seek ambiguity, recognizing that it is often ambiguity that leads to great insights.

"At Walmart," says Fan," inclusive leaders don't just listen, they prime the pump to hear dissenting opinions. In some areas our leaders purposefully assign a devil's advocate while making a big decision," he says. "They'll say: 'No matter what you believe you need to go to the opposite side and argue for the case.' This practice offers us an opportunity for constructive debates to ensure our decision is well-informed and well thought through with various aspects in mind. If everyone just plays a yes-man kind of role, then you can very easily miss diverse perspectives."

It's that kind of nurturing of creative, counter-intuitive thinking that has launched many new and innovative products and companies over the past years.

Some of the most effective inclusive players today have been around for just a very short time.

- Amazon was founded in 1994 (49 on Fortune 500 in 2013)

- Google was founded in 1998 (55 on Fortune 500 in 2013)

- Facebook was founded in 2005 (482 in 2013; first time on list)

Predisposition For Innovation

There's another way of looking at this. In addition to the Fortune 500, Fortune also creates a list of the "World's Most Admired Companies."[16] While the Fortune 10 is comprised largely of legacy oil firms, the most admired companies reflect the innovative climate that has been fueled by technology: Apple, Google and Amazon.com hold the top three spots on the list. Perhaps more interesting, as Geoff Colvin pointed out in "The World's Most Admired Companies: Built for Brilliance,"[17] seven of the top ten on the list are one-person organizations, e.g. Facebook/Zuckerberg and Amazon/Bezos. Thirty years ago, in 1983, only one of the top ten was led by single individual—Digital Equipment. The others were, as Colvin points out: "long-established institutions, corporate aristocracy." It remains to be seen whether these most admired firms will eventually own the top of the Fortune 500 list, but it's probably a safe bet. Today, innovative thinkers rule.

Today's leaders must be able to cultivate, nurture and take advantage of the organic innovation within their organizations. And they must look outside their organizations continually to assess the changing landscape and changing preferences of their current customers while remaining attuned to the potential to reach into new markets. While the top ten on the

---

[16] *World's Most Admired Companies*. (n.d.). Retrieved from http://money.cnn.com/magazines/fortune/most-admired/?iid=EL

[17] *The World's Most Admired Companies: Built for brilliance*. (n.d.). Retrieved from http://money.cnn.com/2013/02/28/news/companies/most-admired-companies.pr.fortune/index.html

Fortune 500 may remain relatively stable—at least to date—the 490 other companies on the list ebb and flow faster than ever before. Those that remain have had to change and grow to meet changing needs—they reflect the Darwinian brain: adapt, migrate, mutate or die.

Effective innovation comes from input. Inclusive leaders must be "intentional" about seeking and acting on input. Senior leaders must be visible, open and explicit about their interest in hearing from people around them—everyone around them. The chain of command can hamper good ideas. Organizations, and their leaders, need to remove these types of barriers to get ideas out. In addition to their own personal efforts to interact and engage with staff, efforts should be made to provide a variety of opportunities for employees to share their thoughts and ideas—through bulletin boards, chat rooms, and other means.

But more than simply seeking input, inclusive leaders have an inclination for action. It's one thing to sit around and think about new ideas. Inclusive leaders are those who are driven beyond the idea to execution —to translating vision into reality. And not just reality. But profitable reality. Their vision must be aligned with the continually shifting needs of the markets they serve. This is possible only through inclusive behavior.

> Inclusive leaders must be able to articulate a vision that people will want to aspire to.
> Rohini Anand
> Sodexo

Inclusive leaders, says Anand of Sodexo, must be able to "articulate a vision that people will want to aspire to." They need to be able to convey: "What is it that we're trying to get to?" "What does an inclusive culture mean?" Perhaps most important, particularly to employees on the front lines: "What does it mean to me, someone who is fairly low down in the organization? How is it going to benefit me?"

IBM is one of those few legacy firms that has managed, despite some setbacks, to maintain a position among the Fortune 100 (it ranked 20th in 2013). Although formally incorporated in 1911, IBM traces its origins back to the end of the 19th century.[18] Leaders at IBM certainly have a predisposition for innovation—the company continues to innovate, despite its legacy nature. Its leaders recognize the value of employees. In a 2013 advertorial, IBM says: "Leading companies aren't just changing the way we work; they're reinventing it. Because when people are more engaged and inspired by their work, they can be more productive and innovative—and ultimately create more value for the companies that employ them."

It's not that long ago that your past could predict your future. The fact that you're on your game today, doesn't guarantee success tomorrow. The inclination toward innovation requires the realization that being innovative is part of the new business normal. Inclusive leaders understand not only the need for continual innovation, but also the sources of information required to allow them to be innovative. They look to user groups, they look to clients, they look to the people who work with them. They actively pursue diverse inputs and they are open to these inputs, not only—but especially—when the inputs may be different from their own perceptions and opinions. It's in that space between the known and the not yet known that innovation can happen. But it happens only if leaders are open to these inputs and are not constrained by their history, their predisposition or their biases. Some simply remain immune or blind to the inputs that surround them.

Inclusive leaders must be driven to seek outcomes. They must <u>have a predisposition for innovation</u>. The predisposition for innovation must also tie into the desire and the ability to remain focused on the market trends that are going to impact

---

[18] *IBM archives: Exhibits.* (n.d.). Retrieved from http://www-03.ibm.com/ibm/history/history/decade_1880.html

their business success. Importantly, inclusive leaders must sometimes go outside the confines of existing cultural norms. For instance, leaders in the Midwest must be prepared to let go of "Midwest nice" if the situation calls for quick, decisive action. Conversely, leaders on the East Coast, who tend to be more direct than their Midwestern counterparts, may need to back off at times. Innovation, in general, only thrives in a culture of inclusiveness, which sometimes requires moving beyond the confines of cultural norms.

Driven to Seek Input

The key to inclusion is employee engagement, says Jorge Quezada, Chief Diversity Officer at Kraft Foods Group, and that means actively seeking input particularly from those who may be less likely to provide it. "What we're trying to accomplish is really three things," he says:

1) We want to make sure that the quietest people in the room know they have a voice

2) We want to make sure that the people who feel like they're the most different in the room feel like they belong

3) Regardless of tenure, we want to make sure that the people in the room feel like they can contribute

It's about listening differently, he says. "I'm listening differently. I'm being more genuine in who I am. I'm focused on greeting people more authentically. I'm making sure that I create a safe environment for people to have a conversation. I lean into discomfort. I bridge ideas better. I want to create an environment where people are participating and are engaged with me so that we can bounce ideas off one another." This is, he says, how organizations effectively leverage innovation. "You're challenging the status quo—that's what innovation is."

Effective teams drive effective companies. Effective companies retain workers. In *What Does Fortune 500 Turnover Mean*, Dane Stangler and Sam Arbesman, with the Ewing Marion Kauffman Foundation, note that performance among the Fortune 500, as measured by return on equity, has become more volatile over time.[19]

Fortune 500 Annual Turnover

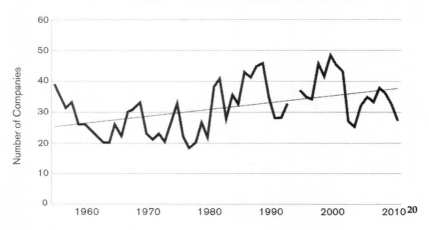

These are more competitive times marked by mergers, acquisitions and market shifts that mean companies move on and off this list on a regular basis. That has always been the case.

But some companies simply go away forever.

In an ad taken out in the *New York Times* by IBM on its 100th anniversary, and referenced in an article by Steve Denning in *Forbes*, we're told that "nearly all the companies our grandparents admired have disappeared. Of the top 25 industrial corporations in the United States in 1900, only two remained on that list at

---

[19] Stangler, D., & Arbesman, S. (2012). *What Does Fortune 500 Turnover Mean?* Ewing Marion Kauffman Foundation. Retrieved from http://www.kauffman.org/uploadedFiles/fortune_500_turnover.pdf

[20] Stangler, D., & Arbesman, S. (2012). *What Does Fortune 500 Turnover Mean?* Ewing Marion Kauffman Foundation. Retrieved from http://www.kauffman.org/uploadedFiles/fortune_500_turnover.pdf

the start of the 1960s. And of the top 25 companies on the Fortune 500 in 1961, only six remain there today."[21]

Each year *24/7 Wall St.* identifies 10 American brands that they believe will disappear over the next year. In 2013, the brands they predict will no longer exist by 2014 are:

- Avon
- MetroPCS
- The Oakland Raiders
- Salon.com
- Suzuki
- Pacific Sunwear
- Research in Motion (the company behind the Blackberry)
- Current TV
- Talbots
- American Airlines[22]

We'll know all too soon how accurate these predictions are. What we know for sure is that a number of iconic brands have faded away over the years. They include: Pan Am, Tower Records, Polaroid, Texaco, Circuit City, DHL and Sharper Image.[23]

"Why did IBM survive?," asks Denning in *Forbes*. His answer: "by listening to clients." We suggest that they also listened to their employees over the past 100 years to continuously change and innovate to meet the needs of a constantly changing

---

[21] Denning, S. (2011, July 10). *Why Did IBM Survive?*. Retrieved from http://www.forbes.com/sites/stevedenning/2011/07/10/why-did-ibm-survive/

[22] McIntyre, D. (2012, June 21). *Ten Brands That Will Disappear In 2013*. Retrieved from http://247wallst.com/2012/06/21/247-wall-st-10-brands-that-will-disappear-in-2013/4/

[23] Felix, S. (2012, October 20). *12 Long-Dead Brands That Are Ripe For Resurrection*. Retrieved from http://www.businessinsider.com/12-dead-brands-that-are-still-well-known-2012-10?op=1

business landscape. To benefit from these inputs, though, organizations must build diverse workforces to ensure that they have the opportunity to capture them from a pool that best reflects their markets.

The moral of the story, says Quezada of Kraft, is "that when you constantly keep diversity and inclusion at the forefront, it allows for alignment to happen much more quickly. You can develop policies and, then, because you're 'all in' for inclusion, you just leverage differences more effectively."

Having diverse teams in your workplace is not enough. It's about nurturing the kind of innovation that is required to sustain and grow your organization. This is particularly critical in a global economy. And, don't kid yourself. Whether or not your business has a global footprint, you are now part of the global economy!

So, it's not only about having diverse teams—it's about listening to those diverse teams, as Anand of Sodexo points out. Leaders, she says, need to ensure that they have diversity in all of their taskforces. "While it may slow down decision-making, at the end of the day you get a better outcome," she says. "It's about ensuring that everyone has a voice at the table. If you have diversity in a leadership room, but you go to the same people every time to hear what they're saying, it's just token diversity. You have to not only bring people to the door, but bring people to the decision-making table which means hearing their voices."

Diverse teams drive more revenue and there is significant research to prove this is the case. For instance, MIT research[24] has demonstrated the bottom line business value of diverse work teams. The issue, though, say researchers is not about what diversity *adds* to a work group, but about what

---

[24] Reid, K. (n.d.). *Why Diversity Matters*. Retrieved from http://web.mit.edu/fnl/volume/195/reid.html

homogeneity *takes away*. What does it take away? It takes away the ability for individuals to understand the complexity of group projects—they assume that others, who look like them, think like them. As a result, blind spots are created. A majority of the participants in the MIT study—1500 research faculty—indicated that having diverse students in their classes improved the overall quality of educational experience. When they next looked at diverse research teams, the benefits continued. The diversity of research teams across a wide range of disciplines increased their understanding of their discipline. More importantly, the diversity of their classroom had reciprocal effects that influenced their view of research.

Anita Williams Woolley of Carnegie Mellon's Tepper School of Business and MIT management professor Tom Malone have found that there is a collective intelligence that predicts a group's overall performance.[25] However, collective intelligence can be undermined where one person dominates the group. Remember command and control? It truly can undermine the wisdom of the team. Another surprise in this study is that researchers noticed groups performed better when women were members of the team. In essence, women tend to demonstrate a higher level of social sensitivity—they're more likely to be inclusive, to let others talk, and to listen. The group's overall effectiveness at cooperating is linked to the number of women in the group!

Another key finding from this research is that the performance of the group is also not directly connected to the individual intelligence of group members. Every member of the group may be a genius, but if they're all the same they don't capitalize on that brain power. IQ isn't as important as diversity of perspectives.

---

[25] Williams Woolley, A., Chabris, C., Pentland, A., Hashmi, N., & Malone, T. (2010, September 30) "Evidence for a Collective Intelligence Factor in the Performance of Human Groups" *Science*. Retrieved from http://www.sciencemag.org/content/330/6004/686.full

Based on studies of hundreds of people working in small groups they identified a "C factor," a statistic that predicts how effectively the group will perform. This factor was more important than the individual IQs of the groups' participants.

An important point to make here within the business context is that soliciting all of these inputs doesn't mean that everyone "gets their way." This is one of the common objections within companies when the issue of being more open and collaborative is raised. Pushbacks generally revolve around concerns that the leader will have to "listen to every harebrained idea." That's not the case. There are, in fact, two important things that leaders can do to help minimize this risk:

- Be crystal clear about the mission and what's important to the organization and make sure that staff are aligned around those critical issues.

- Know when it's time to redirect the conversation and do so in such a way that it doesn't close down future conversations, but simply ensures alignment with the issues that are important to the organization.

It's about maintaining a laser focus on the issue at hand, rather than opening conversations up too broadly. The inclusive leader must set the agenda while bringing all the voices into the room to be heard so the final set of decisions has benefitted from different points of view—even if the final decision is the leader's to make.

Embracing Technology to Fuel Innovation

If there is one significant shift that has impacted managers around the globe and is germane to the success of inclusive leaders, it is the rapid evolution of technology. Technology has changed not only the way products are created and services are delivered, but how we communicate with each other.

Technology has created opportunities and eliminated barriers that previously existed.

As Hoffman of Cisco points out, "technology has helped to open virtual borders and create real time connections, but what many don't think about is that it has also been a significant catalyst to inclusion. Leaders have more tools than ever before to be collaborative, which is the driving force behind mobilizing talent to build inclusion."

That can, of course, be challenging. Hoffman notes one of her biggest fears is "that technology has overtaken humanity. It's critical," says Hoffman, "that the human connection is aligned with the technology connection to allow the 'power of collaboration through inclusion.'"

Technology companies, like Cisco, may arrive at the business case for inclusion more readily. Cisco realized, says Hoffman, that inclusion was embraced as a competitive advantage—the company realized that its industry was shifting and that inclusion could help with these shifts. Like Cisco's leaders, inclusive leaders in other organizations have successfully embraced these shifts, recognizing that there is value in the communication that can come through free-flowing interactions between employees, between customers, between customers and employees—and between the world at large and their organizations. While some non-inclusive leaders have attempted to stem this tide of information fueled by emerging technologies, their more successful competitors have recognized the value in these inputs to drive innovation which leads to business success.

> It's critical that the human connection is aligned with the technology connection to allow the 'power of collaboration through inclusion.'
> Sandy Hoffman
> Cisco

"One of the things that inclusive leaders do is use technology to expedite their communication process," says Fernandez of FedEx Office. "Inclusive leaders are using technology to help them be more inclusive of all generations in the workplace today." Twitter and Facebook are not a waste of time when leveraged for new insights.

At Walmart, says Fan, there is a recognition that as consumer behaviors change, "we need to adapt and select the products that will best meet our customers' needs." Walmart is doing that through the use of technology in ways that may seem counterintuitive. For instance, he says, Walmart has developed a mobile application that consumers can download to their smartphones. The app will recognize the store they are in and give them information on what products are on sale, will let them create and view a shopping list, scan products, provide a total and pay at a self-checkout register when they're done shopping. "Sometimes people just pick up the items they want and never think of what the total price is," says Fan. "The total price could exceed their plan but with this application you know how much is in your basket."

We might think that retailers would be most interested in driving up sales volumes, regardless of the impact on consumers. But, Walmart has taken the long view, recognizing technology not as a threat, but as an opportunity. In fact, says Fan: "We're still looking into adding on different functions or abilities, such as comparing the price with competitors. All of this is really about how we're going to change our business model to adapt to our customers' needs and wants. Be their advocate and provide them the best access and value so they can live better."

Counterintuitive but powerful.

Using technology to facilitate inclusion effectively requires

- the ability to seek information and feedback from various audiences;

- the willingness to act on those inputs, however counterintuitive they may seem; *and*

- a bias for action.

In a fast-moving global environment, responding effectively — and promptly — to feedback coming from stakeholder channels like social media is critical. Fernandez of FedEx Office continues, "In social media today if something goes up and it's not responded to in a timely manner, it can make a difference in a customer or team member relationship. In the work that I do, I make sure that when I get an opinion or recommendation on something, I take action quickly." More and more, opinions are coming from multiple communication channels, such as traditional and emerging media sources. Inclusive leaders need to be vigilant and continually monitor all internal and external communication sources.

"Once you get the information and the feedback from your team or customers, things should roll," says Fernandez. "If you don't, you're going to be judged not on what you say, but what you do."

Different environments prompt different responses. In China, for instance, says Fan, Walmart has purchased one of the biggest e-commerce companies. The company provides technology that allows consumers to browse and scan day-to-day consumption items that may be displayed on billboards in subway stations, for instance. "You just use your iPhone to scan the item to place an order and then, before you get home, the item is delivered at your door." These innovative approaches, he says, are designed to provide exceptional customer experiences.

Inclusive leaders drive organizational success by seeking and valuing these varied technological and social developments, recognizing that the environment is continually changing, and understanding their own blind spots or assumptions.

Inclusive organizations and their leaders understand that the inclusive behaviors and traits are required in this digital age and will be necessary to effect positive change. They need to consider what they're doing to value diverse perspectives and how they are creating a culture that nurtures input and innovation. Importantly, they need to embrace technology— whether they're in the retail space, manufacturing, or service industries.

People and Market Radar:
Thousands of Eyes on the Horizon

There is a certain amount of humility that is required to be open to the input of those around you. The recognition that you are not the smartest person in the room, that you do not have all of the answers, that the very moment when you believe you have achieved success is the moment you are most vulnerable to be picked off by a competitor or unseated by an environmental shift.

Innovation doesn't come just from the C-suite—far from it. Innovation comes from the front lines. The success of companies like Walmart, Microsoft and Amazon is driven not solely by the brilliance of the top leaders—but by their ability to engage the creativity and innovation of every single member of their team.

Inclusive leaders have learned to look outward, rather than inward, for their insights. They are people and market centric. They know they will benefit not from two, but from *thousands* of eyes on the horizon. And they seek those insights proactively.

There are many, many companies in the world today that have taken their eyes off the horizon—they suffer from blind spots that will eventually lead to their downfall. Again, it comes back to leading inclusively. Consider a consumer goods organization with a leadership team comprised entirely of male Baby Boomers. Their market, like many in this space, is dominated predominantly by females. How effective can these leaders be if they're not market-centric but internally driven with insights based only on their own limited perspectives?

Ensuring that your organization has thousands of eyes on the horizon is a four-step process:

1. Creating a culture that embraces and nurtures the value of all input

2. Establishing mechanisms for capturing this input

3. Being transparent about how decisions will be made

4. Communicating the decision, with rationale, back to the key stakeholders

It's about having not only the inclination toward gathering input and listening to all voices, but about putting mechanisms in place so that the phenomenon of the crowd's point of view —internal crowdsourcing—can occur. (More about mechanisms later in this chapter.)

It is also important that the inputs being sought come from those who are most knowledgeable about the markets you are pursuing—either they represent those markets or have a background and history that has made them very attuned to those markets.

The historical disconnect between the internal demographics of an organization and its external constituencies creates the opportunity for evolution to a culture based on an organization's key employee demographics required for growth.

Consciousness and Commitment

"In order for us to really be relevant to our customers, our workforce must reflect who they are and what they think so we know their insights better than the others and we can better serve them," says Fan.

Walmart has been around for 50 years, says Fan. "We started in 1962—it took us 50 years to become the Fortune number one—a business of close to half a trillion dollars. I did the calculation. With the current growth rate, it would take us about another 15 years to become a $1 trillion company. What does that mean? $1 trillion is equal to the GDP of Korea—the 15th largest economy in the world. What kind of workforce will we need to support that size of a business? We will need all kinds of talent across the world. We know that now. And we know we can't wait for 15 years to really address the challenge in front of us." That kind of forward-looking behavior helps Walmart stay ahead of the curve, he says. "If we think in future tense, we get ourselves prepared to thrive tomorrow."

Inclusive leaders know that their organizations' success depends upon comprehensive and integrated approaches that tie directly back to the overall business strategy. The most successful inclusion strategies are consistent, comprehensive, accountable and sustainable. Every CEO wants to see where company-wide initiatives impact the bottom line. Consequently any inclusion efforts must have meaningful and measurable ties back to the overall business strategy and a clear return on investment.

Rather than seeing the differences within companies or working groups as an impediment to cooperation and productivity, savvy companies know that the diversity among their employees is a significant asset.

Valuing Differences—Leveraging Input

The traditional method of running an organization is a very top-down, command and control model. High-level executives determine policy and business strategy and dictate down through the chain of command to the front-line employees. More and more companies, however, are increasingly encouraging and acting on feedback from employees throughout the organization. And for good reason. As businesses continue to seek out and compete for the most qualified, savvy and creative employees from top schools and industry-leading competitors, it only makes sense that they capitalize on those investments as much as possible.

However, simply adhering to the principal that all employees can offer input is not enough if employees do not believe their input is actually valued. Many employees feel they are overstepping their bounds and irritating the higher-ups if they share their opinions on company policy, let alone challenge the prevailing wisdom. It is crucial, therefore, for companies that value input from their employees to create an environment in which those employees are recognized for their ideas— rather than being "punished" for ideas that may challenge the status quo.

Both diversity and inclusion have a place in today's workplace, says Anand of Sodexo. "It's about ensuring that your workplace is diverse, but I don't think that's adequate," she says. "You need an inclusive culture as well; a culture where everyone can bring their whole self to work in order to achieve their fullest potential. You can have an inclusive culture with people who are all the same, but I don't think that benefits the business. You need to have both diversity and inclusion. One without the other is a promise unfulfilled."

If the idea of inclusive leadership is to nurture and leverage the insights from a vast array of individuals, within and outside the organization, then there must be a corresponding commitment to value, recognize and reward these ideas, and those who contribute them.

Key Takeaways

- Inclusive leadership begins with self-awareness—the ability to assess personal strengths as well as opportunities for improvement.

- A pre-disposition toward innovation drives inclusive leaders to seek input from multiple constituencies—both inside and outside their organizations.

- Inclusive leaders are driven to make an effort to draw out the quieter voices around them.

- Having diverse teams is only one aspect of inclusive leadership; success requires the ability to effectively listen to diverse voices. Research shows the bottom-line business value of doing so.

- Changing consumer values, needs and behaviors require inclusive leaders to be agile and adept at meeting these continually shifting demands.

- The fast-moving global environment requires a strong bias toward action.

CHAPTER 4:
BECOMING THE INCLUSIVE LEADER— WHAT YOU CAN DO NOW

If organizational leaders need any evidence that complacency can lead to irrelevance, they need only be handed a videocassette, a floppy disk or an encyclopedia. No, these C-suite leaders, don't have to change. They don't have to adapt to the changing consumer market. They don't have to develop products that the consumer wants. They can simply continue to hold their ground—until they can't anymore.

The problem is that most leaders don't realize that they can't until it's too late. They remain confident, even cocky, while the world changes around them until they are suddenly—and often very publicly—unseated.

While some leaders are fortunate to work within inclusive organizations, most find themselves fighting lonely battles trying to convince senior leaders that inclusion is the answer to combat the brain drain internally and shrinking market externally. Too many senior leaders view inclusion as a diversity initiative—as a soft, non-business focused, endeavor tied to filling positions with women and people of color.

> The inclusive leader and the inclusive organization need to be laser-focused on doing those things that serve the customer and grow the business.
> Shirley Engelmeier
> InclusionINC

The inclusive leader and the inclusive organization need to be laser-focused on doing those things that serve the customer and, consequently, grow the business. Once people understand that the culture is one of "listening and serving," they can get behind that culture because there is alignment between words and deeds. When they see that leaders are aligned around listening and serving they will, in turn, listen and serve.

The Inclusive Leader Continuum

Many potential inclusive leaders find themselves "trapped" in organizations that are not inclusive from the top. There may be pockets of inclusive leaders within the organization, but without a top-down focus, the organization will not be an inclusive one.

Potential mid-level inclusive leaders—don't despair. While the challenges may sometimes seem insurmountable, and it can certainly be personally challenging to exist in an environment or culture that does not reflect your own, change can occur over time. On a micro level, there are things that *you* can do to develop the inclusive traits and behaviors that have been discussed in this book and you can practice those inclusive behaviors with your own work team. On a macro level, you can develop means of modeling and demonstrating the *bottom-line impact* of being an inclusive leader. You can create proof points and measurable outcomes of the value of inclusive leadership through your actions and your successes.

The journey to become an inclusive leader and organization occurs along a continuum that requires self-reflection, honest assessment and a commitment toward change. It's a continuum that involves work and effort but that ultimately leads to "unconscious competence"—acting without effort—the point at which your inclusive behaviors become so second nature that you don't even feel the need to "work" at being inclusive.

Gordon's Four Stages of Competence provides a good model for illustrating the process:

The Four Stages of Competence

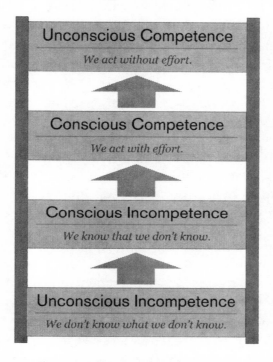

Like any model, though, the process appears more straightforward in an illustration than it is in reality. Changing yourself is hard —really hard. If you're operating in the window where you are "unconsciously incompetent," by definition you *do not know* that you are incompetent. For each of us, what we see is colored through our personal lenses which have developed based on the collective of all of our past experiences, the cultures we were born into, raised in, have worked in and have experienced. That is the lens through which we see the world and interpret the meaning of events.

These personal lenses are by definition flawed, often in ways leaders don't even recognize. For instance, if an employee approaches a leader and says: "This isn't working," it's not uncommon for the leader to view this input as a personal criticism. Inclusive leaders become adept at recognizing their own potential for bias—particularly when their egos are involved—and they are able to more deeply reflect on what they hear, even when what they hear is negative or critical. Inclusive organizations promote an environment of openness to these types of inputs. Employees are encouraged to "speak up and speak out" when they see something that needs to be improved. They take ownership. These are the types of behaviors that inclusive organizations, and their inclusive leaders, must nurture.

As the authors of "Women Rising: The Unseen Barriers" note in *Harvard Business Review*[26]: "Learning how to be an effective leader is like learning any complex skill. It rarely comes naturally and usually takes a lot of practice."

Within your own work teams you can take steps to ensure that your team represents the market you serve. You can ensure that you have created an environment that encourages the open sharing of ideas, insights and even criticism. You can break down hierarchical structures and engage workers at all levels and in all roles, regardless of tenure, in the pursuit of innovation. You can become a role model. You can work as an internal change agent, or catalyst, to drive inclusive behaviors throughout the organization. As you do, you will find allies in your organization, always recognizing that there is strength in numbers—both the numbers of individuals who embrace inclusive leadership and the numbers you can present to your leaders to demonstrate the real, business-related impacts of inclusiveness.

Listen In!

Sheryl Sandberg touched a nerve with her book *Lean In* (Knopf, 2013) and we applaud the fact that she brought forward the topic of women being stalled in their efforts to take on

---

[26] Ibarra, H., Ely, R., & Kolb, D. (2013, September). *Women Rising: The Unseen Barriers*. Retrieved from http://hbr.org/2013/09/women-rising-the-unseen-barriers/ar/1

leadership roles. The same advice she offers to women could be applied to a number of different segments of the workforce.

Despite the fact that she has created awareness around an important topic, she doesn't take the argument far enough. It's not enough just to lean in. Leaning in when there's nobody there to notice, or to catch you, will often result in these eager leaders falling on their faces!

Think about your own organization. Who are you listening to? If it's just the senior leaders, you're missing out. Are you hearing the voices of Gen Y? Of women? Of people of color? Of new employees? If you're not, it really doesn't matter how much they "lean in" does it? Leaning in doesn't accomplish anything if leaders—*inclusive* leaders—aren't also "listening in."

Inclusive leaders must be alert to the leadership potential within their organizations and among the literally thousands of skilled workers knocking on their doors. When someone leans in, organizational leaders need to be there to help guide them!

This isn't rocket science! Yet, far too many organizations—large and small—fail to take one simple step to engage their staff: listen. Listening means actively seeking the input of employees at every level within your organization, regardless of their age, length of service, or position.

Be careful here to ensure that despite your good intentions to be inclusive, you are not inadvertently excluding certain groups. Here are a few examples of the cautions to take:

- As new employees enter your organization and you seek their fresh ideas and insights are you inappropriately dismissing the insights of those who have been on your staff for years? And, conversely, do you minimize the input of new employee because they "need more experience"?

- As you work to reap the input and innovation of Gen Y are you inadvertently overlooking the input of your Baby Boomer employees?

- As you seek to be inclusive of your female audience are you overlooking input that your male audience may have to offer? As you seek customer input do you focus more on new than more long-term customers, or vice versa?

- When you turn your ear to the market are you only picking up on the input of those who are like you and share your opinions and perspectives?

Inclusive leaders recognize areas where their own biases may make them inadvertently shut down input.

"Organizations have to support this self-awareness with an infrastructure that is prepared to effectively 'catch' those who are leaning in," says Hoffman of Cisco. "Companies need to be ready to be leaned on. If you don't have an environment or an infrastructure that supports this, it makes it more difficult." There are, she stresses, "two sides of the equation to open up the conversation. Take a look around your organization. Who's leaning in? Are you poised and prepared to catch them when they do? Secondly, are you actively seeking ways to draw out their input, putting the onus on the organization, rather than the individual, to find opportunities for contribution?"

Listening in means really listening, especially when the things you hear differ from your own viewpoint or perspective; in fact, that's when the most meaningful impacts occur. Listening means providing an infrastructure that offers numerous opportunities for input across communication channels—from face-to-face to technology-driven. And, finally, listening means closing the loop to let employees know that they've been heard and how valuable their ongoing insights and perspective is to the organization.

Moving Beyond "Good Enough"

It's far too easy, and quite common, for organizations to view themselves in light of their competitors and if doing about the same as their competitors they will think: "Well, we're good enough." Inclusive leaders are not "good enough" leaders. They don't settle for less than the best. It's all about the opportunity; it's all about the upside—growth, growth and more growth.

This is where ego strength comes into play. Leaders must have the ability to lay out a clear and strong vision and support a culture that aligns employees with that vision. It's not enough for them to simply make proclamations or post the vision on the wall. They must show, through their own actions, that they live the vision.

The biggest challenge for those who aspire to be inclusive leaders, says Fernandez of FedEx Office, is finding they are in an organization where the culture is not inclusive. "Within organizations, leadership drives organizational values. If you're not onboard with the core principles and culture of the organization, it will be difficult for an individual to be rewarded or acknowledged. Even organizations that have an inclusive leader at the helm may experience leadership changes that can challenge that culture, he says. "I'm fortunate that I work for a company that does value inclusion. I'm able to navigate through the company more strategically and in a timely manner since inclusion and diversity is supported and valued."

"Coming out of this recession there are some companies that instead of ramping up inclusionary practices have scaled them back." Aspiring inclusive leaders, Fernandez says, can address these challenges. "The one thing I've found that's sustainable is tying it back into the business. If you do not have an inclusionary culture, then what you can do is speak to it from the business standpoint. Try to demonstrate how inclusion can lead to better engagement, better productivity, reduced turnover and innovation," says Fernandez.

At the end of the day, says Fernandez, it's results that will get attention and funding. "That's what everybody is looking for in today's work environment. They're looking for better employees, they're looking for better engagement, better productivity and innovation—that's going to help them differentiate themselves from their core competitors.

"At a company I previously worked for we had a scorecard that basically said, we're doing all this great work and here's how it's manifesting itself in terms of results. We were able to demonstrate how much turnover was down and how employee engagement had increased. And ultimately, we ended up coming up with 10 really innovative ideas because we provided our team members with a voice and they told us about some great things that we could do to improve our business." Those are the things that really, at the end of the day, capture the minds —and hearts—of all leaders.

The Need to Create Inclusion Mechanisms

Of course even when leaders possess the traits and exhibit the characteristics of inclusiveness, they must still seek ways, operationally, to mobilize, facilitate and translate inputs. There are a variety of mechanisms that can be used to foster inclusion —tactical steps that inclusive leaders take to ensure that they are finding, listening to, acknowledging and following up on the information they receive. And, furthermore, that they are creating a climate where employees, and customers, feel safe to bring up their viewpoints, especially when those viewpoints may be constructive rather than complimentary.

Some companies exude inclusion and, therefore, attract top talent. FedEx Office is one of those companies, says Fernandez. In fact, says Fernandez, it was the company's inclusive culture that drew him to the organization. "FedEx Office has a diverse and inclusive culture, supported by senior management, which is crucial to the success of the work in these areas," says Fernandez.

But, stresses Fernandez, the case for inclusion needs to be built on business principles. "When you really speak to your leaders about the value of inclusion from a business standpoint and speak to it in business language, that's how you can start to get the buy-in and traction," he says. "In today's environment, it's all about doing things that make a difference and contributing to the organization from a business standpoint."

Inclusive leaders need to focus on business benefits. It's not about "doing the right thing"—it's about doing things that demonstrably, and positively, impact the business and those it serves.

As inclusive leaders like Fernandez recognize, a culture must be built where people know that they have the license to focus their eyes on the horizon, and share insights they're gathering. This can be challenging in an environment where employees, for instance, are focused on getting their work done, or where customers are engaging with multiple organizations every day. Inclusive leaders must create both the environment and the mechanisms for effectively gathering new information in meaningful ways that will lead to measurable actions.

It can be challenging, says Fan of Walmart. "I think a lot of times people will assume that if you have a diverse workforce or diverse team you will immediately reap the value of diversity," he says. That's far from the truth. The reality, he says, is just the opposite. "Whenever you have a diverse team you will have more tension and conflict, and you will spend more time to drive solutions." So, what do inclusive leaders need to do in these situations? They need new competencies, and new tools, to help them navigate this sometimes tricky terrain so they can unlock the synergy that a diverse team provides.

There are a wide range of tools that leaders can use to boost inclusion in their organizations. Some have existed for some time; others have emerged through technological advances and demographic demands. Inclusive leaders can more effectively leverage these tools to ensure they are capturing inputs from all areas, and all members, of their organizations.

Let's look at more tools, such as crowdsourcing, inclusive leadership training, celebration of great ideas, InclusionCIRCLES™, hackathons, internal communities, Kaizens, and skunkworks.

Crowdsourcing

In 1896 when Henry Ford developed the Model T in Highland Park, Michigan, the world felt pretty small and insights were hard to come by. After all, the telephone had only been around for about 20 years and had still not seen widespread adoption. Perspectives were primarily limited to the local community. When Ford decided to offer this new marvel in one color — black — it probably didn't seem all that outrageous. Fast forward 120 years and the world has changed significantly. Today inputs can, and do, come literally from around the globe. No longer are companies able to unilaterally make decisions on behalf of their markets — they must listen to their markets. The result is more choices, improved market share and more satisfied customers.

Crowdsourcing is a term that has sprung up in the Digital Age to refer to the process of soliciting ideas from a large group of people. Inclusive leaders can crowdsource by actively seeking input from employees, for instance, through the use of online forums, live chats or other technology-enabled media. The same process can be used externally. Doritos' "Crash the Super Bowl" campaign[27], for instance, turned to the public to solicit ads that competed to appear during the Super Bowl broadcast. The campaign has been running for six years and has resulted in both PR buzz and sales.

As part of Cisco's ongoing emphasis on Inclusion & Diversity, it launched a company-wide crowdsourcing initiative to help

---

[27] *Doritos crash the superbowl viii.* (n.d.). Retrieved from https://apps.facebook.com/crashthesuperbowl/

validate its strategy and give employees an opportunity to shape the company's vision through technology. Over the course of a week, employees from around the globe submitted over 500 ideas, made over 600 comments, and contributed 5,539 votes on which ideas they preferred. "It was very exciting to see both the high volume of responses as well as the serious thought our employees gave this very important topic. This format allowed us to quickly understand what is most important to our employees, what will resonate with our key stakeholders and allow us to drive the strategy quickly and cost efficiently," says Hoffman. That, she says, "is the future of workplace democracy." Employees don't come to work to be drones or to be a number. They want to be heard; they want a stake in the company."

But large organizations aren't the only ones that can benefit from crowdsourcing. In fact, it could be said that crowdsourcing is the great equalizer, allowing organizations of any size to benefit from the wisdom of the masses. Consider Threadless, a t-shirt company founded by a high school student as a school project. Based on a simple concept—users submit t-shirt designs that are judged by other users, and the winners make it into the store—the company has grown to about 75 people in 2013, 10 years after Jake Nickell launched the project.[28]

Two heads *are* better than one. Thousands—even millions— are infinitely better!

Inclusive Leadership Training

While some leaders certainly have a greater propensity for exhibiting inclusive leadership behaviors than others, it can't be assumed that even these "naturally inclusive" leaders will be able to successfully lead their teams toward better outcomes.

---

[28] MacLary, R. (n.d.). *Threadless uses crowdsourced design ideas for t-shirt success*. Retrieved from http://dailycrowdsource.com/crowdsourcing/ company-reviews/81-threadless-uses-crowdsourced-design-ideas-for-t-shirt-success

Training is necessary to ensure that leaders' actions are aligned with the desired corporate culture and that they have the tools to serve effectively in their roles.

Fernandez is one of the presenters for FedEx's Office Manager Operations Training program. "In the classroom, I emphasize the importance of creating an inclusive and diverse team that really understands the diversity of the consumers in their specific markets. This is critical for continuing to grow and differentiate a business.

"With 1800 centers throughout the country, our leaders in the field are our brand ambassadors," he notes. "Our greatest resource is people. So, if you can get people more engaged by being more inclusive, they will be more innovative and actually produce at a higher level because they feel valued and empowered, and that's something that everybody wants.

"It's important to have inclusive teams in the home office but, if you're really going to be successful, you have to have that message travel all the way down to where the rubber meets the road."

> Building leadership capability is about having genuine conversations, that are safe and that allow leaders to express themselves and be open.
> Jorge Quezada
> Kraft

But, notes Quezada of Kraft, building leadership capability, needs to go beyond training. "The easy answer is to say 'oh, we have this training and we put our leaders through training'—that's easy." What's required, he says, is carrying on the conversation beyond training. Building leadership capability, he says, is about having genuine conversations, that are safe and that allow leaders to express themselves and be open. Often, it means pushing beyond the surface to acknowledge and recognize when maybe they say

"I got it," but they really don't. And then, instead of expressing defeat that they "just didn't get it," engaging in another conversation. "Now you have a data point on where they're at and, when you come back and meet with them again you can continue the conversation."

Yes, it takes time to nurture inclusive leaders. But the effort is well worth it. As the organization's numbers of inclusive leaders grow, so do both internal and external benefits.

Celebration of Great Ideas

Celebrating great ideas may seem obvious. However, celebrating ideas is something that needs to be actively incorporated into a company's culture. Whether that celebration includes tangible benefits such as bonuses, raises and promotions or more subtle perks like public or private recognition or opportunities for employees to have more control over their work, these incentives are crucial in encouraging employees to continuously innovate and to provide signals to the rest of the workplace that great ideas and those who come up with them are highly valued and well-respected.

Foursquare and other innovative 21st century companies are finding creative ways to engage employees through celebration and recognition. [29] For example, Foursquare uses what it calls "Demo Days" to allow staff to show off what they're working on and gather fresh insights from others. Formulated like venture capital pitches, Demo Days are held almost weekly and employees are recognized for their innovations.

InclusionCIRCLES™

InclusionCIRCLES™ are formed on a project basis to solve a problem or to seize an opportunity that is critical to the

---

[29] Gannon, D. (2011, July 19). *How to Reward Great Ideas*. Retrieved from http://www.inc.com/guides/201107/how-to-reward-employees-great-ideas.html

business. Effective InclusionCIRCLES are comprised of a diverse representation of employees including different levels, functions, and years of service. The idea: to bring together diverse people with diverse viewpoints to generate ideas that might have remained dormant without the opportunity for these discussions.

A key component, though, is ensuring that someone within each group has been assigned the role of facilitator and is prepared to ensure that all voices are heard and that even the quietest members of the group provide input. The concept is simple: gather leaders and employees together on a frequent basis, either physically or virtually, to share ideas and address key business issues. They follow core principles to guide the dialogue with a 360° perspective of the issue, the consumer, the employee and the business. Once the business issue is handled, the InclusionCIRCLE is disbanded.

Hackathons

The IT world has popularized the concept of hackathons—events where programmers come together for intense collaboration around a particular project. These events could last anywhere from a day to a week in length. The concept has caught on. Today the concept is used by innovative leaders in many industries as a means of bringing people together to focus their efforts on a specific issue or innovation.

Doubt whether the concept can work? Twitter was created via hackathon by a group of employees working at a company called Odeo, Inc., in San Francisco.[30] The company still uses the concept to fuel innovation, as does Facebook, which believes that hackathons "serve as the foundation for some great (and not so great) ideas." And that's the point. Not everything that

---

[30] Sagolla, D. (2009, January 30). *How Twitter Was Born*. Retrieved from http://www.140characters.com/2009/01/30/how-twitter-was-born/

emerges from a hackathon will represent the next greatest thing. But some things may. And, most importantly, much of the value lies in the process—the bringing together of people with varied perspectives to share those perspectives in an open environment.

Internal Communities

Internal communities, often called Business Resource Groups (BRGs) or Employee Resource Groups (ERGs), are groups of employees with shared backgrounds, interests or characteristics that come together to share perspectives, and gain insights about each other and about their workplaces. But, while ERGs may by their nature seem exclusive, that is far from the case. They are a rich source of information, insight and understanding that anyone within the organization can benefit from on both personal and professional levels.

During his 27 years with Allstate, Quezada recalls that ERGs were great resources for the organization and were often used by leaders to broaden their understanding of different market segments, both internally and externally.

"Employee resource groups, by design, are helping you brand the company, helping you in talent acquisition, helping you in community involvement and helping you develop employees. But, what they also do is create a kind of 'hive' where affinities come together allowing you to learn about other people more readily."

Kaizens

Kaizen is a Japanese word which means good (zen) change (kai). It's a philosophy that was picked up by companies like Toyota in quality management and continuous improvement efforts. For inclusive leaders, the use of Kaizen is tied directly to the value of leveraging employee insights and inputs to make positive change.

Toyota has indicated that the use of Kaizen in their production plant required

- that workers be asked to share their ideas for improvement;

- that diverse groups were assembled to solve problems; *and*

- that participants and workflow stopped to conduct brainstorming and immediate fixes.

Every employee in an organization is welcome to participate in Kaizen and all are encouraged to come up with suggestions. These are typically not "big ideas," but small, incremental improvements.

An important point that Toyota has made relative to the use of Kaizen and the philosophy of actively soliciting employee input is that this is not a philosophy that leads to chaos. Input is still sought in an environment of order and structure. The use of Kaizen does not mean that "anybody can start doing things in his or her way." This is often a concern for managers who are new to the idea of involving and engaging employees.

There are a number of companies that have used Kaizen including Ford, Intel, Lear, Lockheed Martin, Maytag, Pella and Sandia Labs.[31]

Kaizen is a building block of the Lean process, an approach traditionally used to streamline manufacturing with a focus on end user or customer needs. Kaizen is about simplicity. As employees from all areas of an organization come together to focus on improving a process, they identify areas where waste could be eliminated. Kaizen events are designed to produce strategies that can be quickly implemented. Outcomes are

---

[31] *Companies Using Kaizen.* (2006, January). Retrieved from http://www.vitalentusa.com/learn/kaizen_list.php

measured and follow-up is done to ensure that gains are sustained over time.

Skunkworks

A skunkworks project is a fast-track initiative in which a work group is created and tasked with working independently on a specialized project that is typically highly innovative. The idea is to allow the loosely organized team to escape the strictures and cumbersome bureaucracies of the larger organization in order to more efficiently and quickly innovate. Lockheed Martin takes credit for the origination of the term Skunk Works (and has even registered the phrase) back in 1943.[32]

Skunkworks projects can be used by businesses to allow employees the opportunity to be creative and take risks without excessive oversight or process, while at the same time maintaining the hierarchical management structure that is needed to run the overall organizations. For example, Google gives engineers 20% of their time to seek out innovative projects on their own.

Skunkworks teams are part of a legacy in major technology firms where the innovation may evolve from an independent team.

---

[32] *Skunk works®*. (n.d.). Retrieved from http://www.lockheedmartin.com/us/aeronautics/skunkworks.html

Key Takeaways

- Inclusive leadership occurs across a continuum; the Four Phases of Competence ladder can serve as a useful model for identifying success.

- The concept of "leaning in" is important, but of little value unless organizations—and their leaders—are prepared to "listen in."

- Leaders must be constantly cognizant of areas of their leadership style that may be "unconscious," a significant challenge but one that can be overcome.

- An important step toward inclusive leadership is refusing to accept "good enough." Refusing to embrace the status quo can help leaders move toward higher levels of self, and organizational, awareness.

- There are a variety of tools, or mechanisms, leaders can use to boost their inclusiveness and ensure relevant input from internal and external groups.

CHAPTER 5:
INTERNAL BENEFITS

The charge for inclusive leaders is to successfully engage and motivate those who have been brought together to further an organization's mission, vision and goals. These individuals, as we have already seen, represent a myriad of backgrounds, experiences and perspectives. Inclusive leaders are those who can effectively harness this diversity to drive organizational success. There are many benefits that may ensue. Employee engagement is a concept that has become increasingly important to organizations and their leaders in the 21st century. Unfortunately, studies show that most are not successfully engaging employees to contribute to their goals. Inclusive leaders have a pivotal role to play here.

In 2013, Aon Hewitt released "2013 Trends in Global Employee Engagement," indicating that, worldwide, 4 out of 10 employees are still not engaged. Importantly, they indicate, employee engagement is a leading indicator of company growth.[33]

The implications to organizations and their leaders are significant. Without engaged employees organizations are challenged with retention issues and at risk of declining productivity, as increased turnover can lead to lower morale, lower productivity and—ultimately—poor business performance. For certain industries, the risk is even greater.

Consider the current 10 hardest jobs to fill in America. They are:

- Skilled trades
- Engineers
- IT staff

---

[33] (2013). *2013 Trends in Global Employee Engagement*. Aon Hewitt. Retrieved from http://www.aon.com/attachments/human-capital-consulting/2013_Trends_in_Global_Employee_Engagement_Highlights.pdf

- Sales representatives
- Accounting and finance staff
- Drivers
- Mechanics
- Nurses
- Machinists/machine operators
- Teachers[34]

The question is: What are you doing to attract and <u>retain</u> skilled workers in these positions?

If you don't know and are worried about the potential you have to engage the best and the brightest, you're not alone. The ManpowerGroup's 2013 report, "The Great Talent Shortage Awakening: Actions to Take For a Sustainable Workforce," indicates that this is a concern that's being felt globally—and that has been for quite some time. Further, they concluded, the greater the talent shortage, the greater the perceived impact on the organization.

Inclusive leadership has a marked impact on both recruitment and retention. Inclusive leadership also drives productivity and innovation.

In an environment where certain skills are in high demand, employees with those skills have a myriad of choices when it comes to employment options. Those in-demand employees are not likely to choose to work for organizations that are not inclusive—that do not actively seek their opinions and put those opinions to use. Organizations that find themselves lacking bench strength when it comes to inclusive leadership traits will be challenged to compete with those that have selected, coached, developed and rewarded leaders that exhibit inclusive behaviors.

---

[34] Smith, J. (2012, May 29). *The 10 Hardest Jobs to Fill in America.* Retrieved from http://www.forbes.com/sites/jacquelynsmith/ 2012/05/29/the-10-hardest-jobs-to-fill-in-america-2/

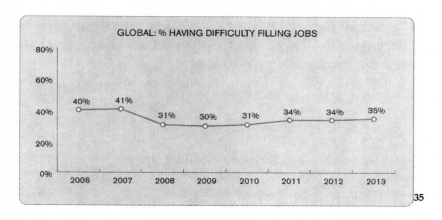

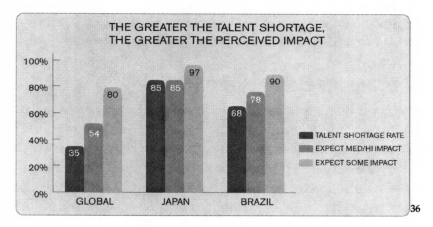

What are you doing to create an ecosystem that ensures your employees are sharing their innovative ideas with you to improve products, services and service to customers and clients?

---

[35] (2013). *The Great Talent Shortage Awakening: Actions to Take for a Sustainable Workforce*. Milwaukee: Manpower Group. Retrieved from http://www.manpowergroup.us/campaigns/talent-shortage-2013/pdf/2013_Talent_Shortage_WP_FNL_US_lo.pdf

[36] (2013). *The Great Talent Shortage Awakening: Actions to Take for a Sustainable Workforce*. Milwaukee: Manpower Group. Retrieved from http://www.manpowergroup.us/campaigns/talent-shortage-2013/pdf/2013_Talent_Shortage_WP_FNL_US_lo.pdf

Inclusive leaders are the answer to dismal employee performance and the mass exodus of talent. Through their efforts they can ensure that organizations are able to

- attract the best and the brightest;

- retain these key employees;

- maintain a productive workforce; *and*

- generate new, innovative ideas.

These efforts go beyond "nice to do." Inclusive leadership is a requisite element of successful businesses in the 21st century. These efforts drive real, sustainable results and growth.

The Internal Benefits Are Real

There are real, measurable benefits of the impact of inclusive leadership. In 2006 for instance, Prudential embarked on an initiative to ensure that its managers appropriately understood differences among employees and that they had the skills and leadership competencies to engage those employees effectively. They were able to demonstrate a return on investment of 320 percent based on a first year savings of more than $800,000 from reductions in turnover and a benefit-to-cost ratio of 4.1 to 1.[37] How? By recognizing the importance of ensuring that the faces of their market are reflected in the faces of their employees —their Key Employee Demographics Required for Growth™. What part of that trillion dollar Latino market do you want? What part of that $30 trillion global market do you want?

As much as many leaders can feel challenged to understand all the various cultures represented in their workforce, it's not hard to be inclusive. It's not that complicated.

---

[37] *Show Us The Money*, Edward E. Hubbard, 3/13/11

Today's employees want their leaders to

- ask their opinions about their work;

- acknowledge their contributions;

- inform them about decisions that will impact their work;

- let them know the "rules of the game"; *and*

- thank them for the work that they do.

Yet, too often, these things do not occur. Instead employees feel that their inputs don't matter or aren't appreciated; that what they think isn't valued by the organization. That, no matter how many times they raise their hands or share an idea, their efforts will be a waste of time. The result: they shut down.

Inclusive leadership skills and behaviors are critical here. Whose voices do most leaders typically ignore or attempt to silence? Those whose perspectives are different from the norm. Whose voices have the potential to drive the organization to unique insights? Those whose perspectives are different from the norm. Inclusive leaders recognize that they must exercise cultural humility and cultural agility to ensure that they are not losing the value of these inputs.

Inclusive leaders must strike a balance between task and human needs. This can be a very delicate balancing act. And, unfortunately, in many companies still today the balance is not present. Many leaders frankly do not care about how people feel. Why? Because they don't perceive any reason to care. Many continue to bask in their current success remaining blind to the realities that threaten them. They are comfortable with the operating assumptions and, in many cases, they continue to be run by Baby Boomers whose cultural leanings are more toward "toughing it out" than being coddled. *They* toughed it out on their way to the top so, naturally, others should do the same.

How can we be alert to situations where we need broader inputs? Inclusive leaders' antennae need to go up when, for instance, they look around the room and see only one Latino participating in a discussion of how to capture more of the Latino market. Their antennae need to go up when they look around the room and see an entirely U.S.-centric group of leaders talking about expanding into China.

Today's leaders must be focused on the needs of their employees to increase engagement and foster loyalty, especially in those areas where talent is increasingly hard to find.

As Fernandez of FedEx Office says, "Our greatest resource is people. So, if you can get people more engaged by being more inclusive, getting people to be more innovative and to actually produce at a higher level because you're an inclusive leader, then that's something that everybody wants."

> Our greatest resource is people. So, if you can get people more engaged by being more inclusive, getting people to be more innovative and to actually produce at a higher level because you're an inclusive leader, then that's something that everybody wants.
> Manny Fernandez
> FedEx Office

Boosting Employee Engagement

As the economy picks up, employee engagement has risen to the top of leaders' agendas across the country. What can these organizations do to ensure that employees remain committed, loyal and productive as their options increase? Inclusive leadership can drive that commitment, says Anand of Sodexo.

"It's about creating a culture where everyone can be successful —that's what an inclusive culture is. It's about understanding what motivates different people—whether it's different generations, or women, or abilities, or sexual orientation or races…whatever the difference might be." That includes, she says, being attentive to things like flexible work arrangements —which, she notes, impact both men and women in today's workplaces.

Inclusive leaders know that their challenge is not simply getting people in the door; it's about keeping them on board. "People are realizing that just because you bring people in doesn't mean they're going to stay," says Quezada of Kraft. "There's a leaky bucket associated with this. So, you have to think about your environment and the environment is about inclusion."

The news about employee engagement, overall, has been dismal so far in the 21st century and there are few signs that we are turning the corner. Gallup has been conducting an ongoing study of the American workplace since 2000 and monitoring trends to provide insights into what leaders can do to improve engagement and, ultimately, performance. Interestingly, over the 13 years of their research, there has been no statistically significant shift in the numbers. We are not making progress!

Failing to engage employees leads to real bottom-line impacts, says Fan of Walmart. "According to the Gallup study, released recently, 70 percent of American workers reported they are either "not engaged" or "actively disengaged. You tie that percentage to the loss of productivity and quantify it with a dollar sign, that's $450-550 billion a year." That loss, he notes, rivals Walmart's annual revenue of $469 billion in 2012. "If you truly have an inclusive environment, or you practice inclusive leadership, then your employees will be highly engaged and you will mitigate that loss." When you frame that argument with real numbers, he says, it's the kind of information that "will capture the CEO's attention."

Building the Business Case for Inclusive Leadership

It is sadly true that most senior leaders in the U.S. today are really not too concerned about being inclusive. They view inclusion as a "code word" for diversity and don't recognize that inclusion is about far more than building a diverse workforce—it's about culture change. Inclusion is a *business imperative*. Unfortunately, until these leaders experience a pain point—the loss of a key employee or customer or the loss of market share to a competitor—they continue to do more of the same.

Other countries around the world are also experiencing these pain points. In India and China for instance, they are losing one-fourth of their workforce through turnover. That's a significant problem. We know that the cost of turnover is significant. Here in America we haven't reached that pain point—yet. But with studies indicating that engagement continues to be low and the certainty that the Baby Boomers *will* eventually leave the workforce, that time may be near. When that and other impacts are felt, those that have been able to achieve internal benefits from their inclusive leadership will also see significant external benefits that will allow them to survive and thrive in the 21st century.

Inclusive leaders can build a business case for inclusion quite readily. One key area where organizations can realize significant advantage from both a financial and cultural perspective is retention. As the economy improves and long-anticipated retirements begin to take place, there will be increasing competition for skilled workers. Organizations with leaders that practice inclusive behaviors—that create cultures where people feel engaged, where they're allowed to contribute and where they feel valued—will be able to demonstrate real, bottom-line impacts. Organizations can readily put a real, monetary value on the loss of productivity and cost involved in bringing new people on board when someone leaves. That cost increases exponentially as turnover rates grow.

Another tangible benefit of inclusion: innovation. Inclusive organizations see broader and wider innovation in the form of process improvements, product development, new customers and new markets. More voices at the table mean better and stronger solutions and, ultimately, better revenue and more profits.

Inclusive organizations thrive on good ideas. Inclusive leaders know that a culture that encourages employees to get those good ideas out is a culture that sees positive impacts.

For example, during a recent class that Fernandez was presenting to center managers, an issue came up related to opportunities with the Hispanic consumer. He noted the opportunities that were raised, connected with one of the FedEx Office VPs, and they both re-connected with the class—that same day—to hear more. "We said, 'listen, we heard these opportunities you brought to us and we want to talk to you a little bit more.'" Then, says Fernandez, "we acted upon their input in less than 24 hours and we came back to them with solutions for these opportunities that had to do with being more inclusive of the Latino customers in specific markets." That ability to be immediately responsive—to follow up—is critical, he says. Unfortunately, in many companies, that follow-up is lacking.

Rather than seeing the differences within companies or working groups as an impediment to cooperation and productivity, savvy inclusive leaders know that the diversity among their employees is a great asset. Diversity within the workplace— whether it be diversity in terms of age, race, sex, socio-economic background or industry experience—offers a company a wealth of knowledge and experiences with which to determine the best strategies to help its business grow and thrive.

Many companies go out of their way to recruit and mobilize a diverse workforce because they genuinely value the benefits a diverse culture can offer their organization. You should too.

Key Takeaways

- "Employee engagement" continues to be top of mind as studies show its steep decline across all industries.

- Regardless of the economy, many knowledge workers are hard to replace—inclusive leaders must take steps to engage their employees to promote retention.

- There are measurable impacts of inclusive leadership.

- When leaders view inclusion as a code word for "diversity" they fail to take advantage of opportunities to ensure that their entire workforce is engaged.

- Diversity (aka "differences") is an asset that can be effectively leveraged by inclusive leaders to boost recruitment, retention and the generation of great ideas from employees.

CHAPTER 6:
EXTERNAL BENEFITS

Some leaders are dragged kicking and screaming into the new normal of the 21st century. A leader with a consumer goods company, for instance, said that they had "no plans to go global" until the recession hit and then "were going out of business if we didn't go global."

We have only to look at the Kodaks, Blockbusters and Tower Records of the world to know that the environment can change significantly in the blink of an eye. Companies that are viable today may be gone tomorrow. Smart leaders—inclusive leaders—know that they too could be impacted by shifts in the market that they had not even anticipated.

Consider how companies today are responding (or not) to the phenomenon of "showrooming"—consumers visiting retail outlets but then going online to make purchases, often through competitive companies. Consider the potential impact that innovations like 3D printing may have on the manufacturing industry, or how healthcare reform will impact the healthcare industry. Consider the phenomenal growth of companies like Fuhu—creator of the award winning nabi® tablet designed for children—and FederalConference.com—an event planning service used by the federal government, topping Inc. Magazine's list of the fastest growing companies in America.[38]

Not enough businesses are yet feeling the pain. Some continue to bask in the confidence of their past success, failing to stay attuned to the very real—and very disruptive—changes occurring all around them.

---

[38] *The 2013 Inc. 5000 List.* (n.d.). Retrieved from http://www.inc.com/inc5000/list/2013

Inclusive leaders can help organizations reposition to address these changes successfully. Being an inclusive leader and staffing your organization (and board rooms) with inclusive leaders holds a number of external, or market, benefits.

Aligning With Markets to Drive Bottom Line Success

Inclusive behaviors have an impact on the kinds of products and services that enter the market place. From a product development and service enhancement standpoint, these inclusive behaviors support close connections with, and a close understanding of, market needs and preferences. That means getting close to the market. Businesses don't achieve success by "buying knowledge." Attempting to "buy" knowledge creates a predatory, rather than an authentic relationship.

Not being predatory requires establishing strong relationships —literally "showing up" in communities. The importance of "showing up" is often underestimated by leaders who are disconnected from the markets they serve. That disconnect leads to faulty understanding. This doesn't occur only in those organizations that are expanding into global markets— disconnects occur domestically as well. When organizations, finding their domestic markets saturated, turn to global markets they generally spend time doing whatever they can to better understand that market. The same approach can, and should, be used when expanding right here in the United States. How much do you really know about the markets you serve? How much more could you learn?

Viewing cultural groups within the U.S. as emerging markets with the potential to grow your business can lead to new insights and new behaviors. It's not the business processes that change, but the business behaviors—the perspective of how the organization will interact with new, domestic, emerging markets. For most organizations there continues to be tremendous opportunity for domestic growth, particularly in the melting pot economy that is emerging.

Consider, for example, the population of California, which has a very large Latino population. If you're a company that operates in California, how well do you understand that Latino market? What have you done to expand your understanding and awareness of what this segment of the population values? Have you actually, physically, gone out into these communities. Have you interacted with those you hope to serve? Have you held focus groups? Have you turned inward to gain insights from your own employees who may be Latino? These are the kinds of actions you might take when expanding globally — they are the same actions that you should take as you seek to expand locally.

Yes, some organizations continue to focus on diversity. But that's a short-sighted approach that often stops short of recognizing the value that diversity brings. It's not simply about having a diverse employee population. The value of diversity — and inclusion — goes beyond social justice. Inclusion — and inclusive leadership — is a business imperative. That means both internally and externally.

Productivity, innovation and success happen when organizations embrace the entire consumer, the entire market. To do this, leaders must effectively understand those consumers. That means achieving alignment between the internal (employee) constituents and the external (customer) markets. We call this Key Employee Demographics Required for Growth™.

Key Employee Demographics Required for Growth™

Individuals, and organizations, says Quezada of Kraft, have a tendency to views issues linearly, left to right. Focusing on inclusion, he says, "forces you to think right to left, starting with business outcomes." For example, he says, in the traditional world of diversity initiatives the focus was on the front end, on hiring certain types of people to meet hiring goals. "I think companies made a classic mistake in saying 'we need to increase our representation by X' and so they'd go out and bring in talent just because of a last name, or a geography, they thought the talent would be culturally sensitive. But the talent hadn't spent the time in the market we were trying to attain. They weren't culturally sensitive to know what was going on."

Now, he says, companies are more frequently looking to determine what kind of markets they serve, or wish to serve. "It just makes you think differently about what your outcome needs to be and how you need to support that outcome," he says.

This is where a company's Key Employee Demographics Required for Growth™ can guide strategy. It means aligning who works in your organization with the markets you serve, and the needs in those markets, and ensuring that these demographics are in alignment. As you look around your organization, are you seeing a mix of people that represent your market? If not, you're hurting your business. Forward-looking leaders will also be considering: "who will we serve," recognizing that changing shifts in the external environment create new opportunities, along with new challenges. Successfully understanding Key Employee Demographics Required for Growth creates a foundation for an integrated, multi-year strategy to align metrics, activities, behaviors and relationships with internal and external stakeholders.

Not all organizations have been, or will be, prepared to deal with the massive shifts occurring around them largely because the historical focus has been on the gender and ethnicity aspects of diversity. The failure to take a broader view—based on inclusion—has caused some significant leadership surprises in terms of ensuring the workplace was poised to address changing needs. Many, says Quezada, "were hit like a ton of bricks" by the Millennials, for instance, or by the disability issues that have emerged as veterans returned to the workforce. "Because their thought processes were around gender and ethnicity, they didn't prepare on the emerging issues."

This is why inclusive leadership is different. Inclusive leadership requires looking beyond your current customers and asking an entirely new set of questions:

- Who are your emerging customers; where are your growth opportunities?

- What are each of those group's needs, values, preferences?

- How can you mine the diverse inputs of our workforce to align with these needs, values and preferences?

- How do customers access our products/services?

- How can you effectively communicate with our customers?

- How can you customize our products and services based on demand?

- And, finally, who needs to work here to successfully sell our products and services?

Let's talk about global growth. In 2012, an article in *McKinsey Quarterly* indicates that, by 2025, a massive wave of urbanization around the world will inject nearly $25 trillion into the global economy. More than 400 emerging-market cities will account for almost half of the expected global GDP growth between 2010 and 2025.[39]

McKinsey's report—*Unlocking the Potential of Emerging-Market Cities*—says that the "massive wave of urbanization" is "shifting the world's economic balance to the east." Nearly $25 trillion

---

[39] Dobbs, R., Remes, J., & Schaer, F. (2012, September). *Unlocking the potential of emerging-market cities.* Retrieved from http://www.mckinsey.com/insights/winning_in_emerging_markets/unlocking_the_potential_of_emerging-market_cities

will be found in emerging-market cities. Yet few leaders, they note, are prepared to focus on this opportunity.

Many CEOs say that, while they understand the opportunity, they are "vexed" about what to do about it.[40] Why? Because all too frequently, rather than capitalizing on the innovation and expertise found among local nationals, they instead take the step of transplanting people just like them to open markets in global locations.

So, if you're hoping to expand operations in Brazil, you need insights from native Brazilians or, at a minimum, someone with an intimate understanding of the Brazilian marketplace. If you're creating products for Gen Y, then your R&D team should include Gen Y and not be populated entirely by Baby Boomers and Gen Xers.

Key Employee Demographics Required for Growth™ Consciousness

Different from filling quotas and meeting legal requirements or representation metrics, it's the consciousness of considering *why* you need diverse viewpoints to help drive your business in ways that will help boost the bottom line. It's not for legal reasons. Inclusion is a business strategy to sell more goods and services and to better serve your markets.

And it's not enough to just *hire* identified demographic categories. Those hired must be retained and their inputs must be sought and listened to. That requires ongoing leadership efforts to ensure engagement and alignment around the key issues that impact the organization.

---

[40] Atsmon, Y., Child, P., Dobbs, R., & Narasimhan, L. (2012, August). *Winning the $30 trillion decathlon: Going for gold in emerging markets.* Retrieved from http://www.mckinsey.com/insights/strategy/winning_the_30_trillion_decathlon_going_for_gold_in_emerging_markets

Here's an example: A multi-national law firm in New York was experiencing trouble retaining top female attorneys. The company decided that, given its market, keeping top female attorneys was an important priority. Programs were created within the firm to specifically address the unique needs of female attorneys. The initiative stemmed from the recognition among senior management that women provided unique and diverse perspectives needed in their business strategy. To retain these key players, the firm instituted a number of programs including alternative work hours, custom work tracks, on-ramping for women coming back from maternity leave and a variety of resource groups.

Each organization will have specific needs to address among its key populations. The first step, though, is identifying what those key populations are based on current and projected market needs. The next step is working to build an inclusive culture from the inside out.

When you're thinking about Key Employee Demographics Required for Growth, you need to consider the changes this might require in your leaders and workforce. This isn't an HR mandate—it's a leadership mandate. The old notion that leaders turn to HR to "go find us some people" doesn't reflect the reality of the workplace and the key role that leaders play in ensuring that those people, once on board, remain engaged. We know that people leave their managers—not their companies. If you're not already actively engaged in the pursuit of key talent, the retention of key talent, and the *engagement* of key talent, it's time to get on board with the notion that your leadership style matters. Using the lens of how your organization defines its Key Employee Demographics

> This isn't an HR mandate—it's a leadership mandate.
> Shirley Engelmeier
> InclusionINC

Required for Growth, your leadership must survey the landscape to determine what sorts of insights you need now—and in the future—to meet business needs.

Inclusive leaders recognize that market intelligence reigns supreme as an input for decision-making. They have to be acutely alert to workforce changes that may threaten market awareness. For instance, it is the inclusive leader who must sound the alarm and say: "Wait a second, that's the third Latino we've terminated here and that's one of our focus markets. We have a problem. We can't serve those markets well if we don't include Latino voices guiding our strategy." It is not an HR issue. It is a leadership issue.

This is how the concept of Key Employee Demographics Required for Growth comes to bear in organizations around the country and, literally, around the world. If you're attempting to serve a growing Gen Y market, you'd better have Gen Y representation among our workforce. You'd also better have some multicultural Gen Y representation. For each organization and for each region, the demands of a customer-centric business environment require that you tailor Key Employee Demographics Required for Growth. If you're attempting to expand globally into new geographies, you'd better be recruiting from those geographies, not just putting our U.S.-centric leaders into those countries.

Embracing a New Way of Thinking

In most organizations, HR is considered to be "in charge of" hiring. But that's backwards thinking and it's the kind of thinking that too often does not serve to improve the business. Most of the time, those in HR are not included in major strategy discussions. What does HR usually know about the organization's markets if they are not included? What does HR usually know about the organization's strategic objectives if they are not a part of the strategy team? What does HR usually know about the business case for being inclusive? Not the need to be legally compliant or to fill quotas, but the bottom line business impacts that can be achieved through inclusive hiring?

Inclusive hiring starts with a clear understanding of both the markets served today and the markets that will be served in the future. It requires a solid understanding of not only the professional skills and background that applicants will bring, but the *cultural* attributes of applicants that *align with* these key target audiences. For a global market that may mean requiring key staff members to speak two or more languages. It may mean requiring key staff to have intimate knowledge of the population served, whether that means they're a native to that population or they've lived within that population and know the culture, characteristics and needs of the audience very, very well.

The shift in thinking goes hand in hand with operating effectively in a global economy. One major global organization recently announced that any individual in any major position in their corporate headquarters must be bilingual and must have worked in another country. Sadly, not all leaders met these requirements. These shifts can be troubling, particularly for leaders who have served organizations long and well and got comfortable with the status quo. But, in these dynamic times, organizations must be focused on attracting, hiring and retaining staff members—especially in key leadership positions—whose views, perspectives and backgrounds can continuously provide them with key insights about their markets.

Key Takeaways

- Internal alignment with external demand is a *leadership* imperative, not an HR responsibility.

- A focus on Key Employee Demographics Required for Growth will help to ensure that internal demographics are aligned with external demand.

- Legacy organizations, still seeing acceptable results, have been slow to change; the failure to scan the environment to identify potential impacts can mean their demise. Some have already felt these impacts.

- It's all about meeting changing market needs—to do that effectively organizations must be equipped to fully *understand* their markets.

- Nurturing a culture of inclusion requires leaders to aggressively seek inputs from those closest to their customers.

CHAPTER 7: TRAILBLAZERS—EARLY ADOPTERS OF INCLUSIVE LEADERSHIP PRACTICES

In an industrial society, non-inclusive behaviors may have generated results but that was then. This is now. In a knowledge-based and knowledge-driven economy, inclusive leadership is now a necessity.

"If you think about it, in the past century it was all about command and control because the characteristic of that era was mass production," notes Fan at Walmart. "You tried to maximize your production line to achieve efficiencies. In that environment process was very important. You needed to have a very well-developed process to drive outcomes." But, in today's information age, organizations are transitioning from command and control to more matrix-driven structures. "The reason for that is the evolution from mass production to individualized demand," he says. "In the old days, for our industry—the retail industry—we said 'whatever we bring, our customer will buy.' Today they are the ones really telling us what they want, and how, when and where they want it. Our industry is transitioning from brick-mortar to multi-channels, including e-commerce and mobile-commerce. The changes in the last 5 years in retail were greater than over the past 50 years. That pace won't slow

> Our industry is transitioning from brick-mortar to multi-channels, including e-commerce and mobile-commerce. The changes in the last 5 years in retail were greater than over the past 50 years. That pace won't slow down moving forward.
> Donald Fan
> Walmart

down moving forward."

Mining Market Nuances

GM sells more cars in China than any other auto manufacturer in large part because it has paid attention to the nuances of the market as it offers new products. For example, the Chevrolet Sail offers an extra-large back seat to accommodate drivers in China who like to offer rides to friends and family. GM also introduced an eight-seat multipurpose van in India where larger families appreciate the roomy comfort.[41]

At Kaiser Permanente, which ranked No. 3 in the 2013 DiversityInc Top Companies for Diversity, then-COO Bernard Tyson (named CEO on July 1, 2013) reported directly to Kaiser's chairman and CEO George Halvorson, an outspoken proponent of diversity and inclusion, particularly as it relates to healthcare disparities. Kaiser also boasts a diverse board of directors and senior management. Importantly, they note that this focus has led to business growth.[42]

A business focus also drives Sodexo, No. 1 on the 2013 DiversityInc list and a leader in the use of diversity metrics to quantify and impact business goals. At Sodexo, commitment and accountability start at the top with President and CEO George Chavel at the helm. Executive-level bonuses are driven, in part, by diversity objectives. This focus is a business necessity

[41] *China Dictates Design as GM Sail Big Back Seat Goes Global: Cars.* (2012, January 13). Retrieved from http://www.businessweek.com/news/2012-01-13/china-dictates-design-as-gm-sail-big-back-seat-goes-global-cars.html

[42] *Diversity & Inclusion Puts Kaiser Permanente on Top With Employees, Customers.* (n.d.). Retrieved from http://www.diversityinc.com/diversity-events/what-makes-kaiser-permanente-no-1-for-diversity/

as Sodexo operates in 36,000 client locations globally. The diversity of their market is immense.[43]

"Diversity has become a differentiator for us," acknowledges Anand. "It has become part of our brand promise." That has positioned Sodexo as a leader among both clients and employees. It is not uncommon, says Anand, to be approached by potential employees who say: "I want to work for Sodexo because you are an organization committed to diversity... but what do you do again?" They know that Sodexo is different. So do Sodexo's clients. Our inclusive culture, she says, is driven by committed inclusive leaders.

There are a number of other CEOs who are recognized as inclusive leaders. They include:

- André Wyss, Novartis Pharmaceuticals Corporation
- John Bryant, Kellogg Company
- Michelle Lee, Wells Fargo
- Steve Howe, Ernst & Young
- John Lechleiter, Eli Lilly and Company
- Arne Sorenson, Marriott International
- Steve Price, Dell
- Mark Clouse, Kraft Foods[44]

Of course, not all organizations—not all leaders—have fully embraced inclusion. Barriers still exist. In a *Harvard Business Review* article, "Great Leaders Who Make the Mix Work,"[45] Boris Groysberg and Katherine Connolly asked CEOs what

---

[43] *Sodexo: No. 1 in the DiversityInc Top 50*. (n.d.). Retrieved from http://www.diversityinc.com/sodexo/

[44] *8 CEOs Whose Inclusive Styles Change Corporate Cultures*. (n.d.). Retrieved from http://www.diversityinc.com/leadership/8-ceos-whose-inclusive-styles-change-corporate-cultures/

[45] Groysberg, B., & Connolly, K. (2013, September). *Great Leaders Who Make the Mix Work*. Retrieved from http://hbr.org/2013/09/great-leaders-who-make-the-mix-work/ar/2

they perceived to be the biggest obstacle facing women in their quest to advance within companies or industries. "If there's a single barrier that affects all women, it's exclusion from networks and conversations that open doors to further development and promotion," they say. The same can be said for other under-represented groups. Not having access to the "movers and the shakers" within organizations or industries is a significant barrier.

The Role of the Trailblazer

"Trailblazers need to set the stage for an inclusive environment from the top down," says Hoffman. At Cisco, she says, "It was pretty easy to get buy-in." Cisco is fortunate to have a CEO who embraces inclusion and exhibits it through his behaviors and actions. He spends many of his days walking the front lines; listening to employees on a regular basis. "If our CEO and senior leadership team didn't buy into this, it wouldn't work," she says. "It has to be embedded in everything that you do."

> If our CEO and senior leadership team didn't buy into this, it wouldn't work. It has to be embedded in everything that you do.
> Sandy Hoffman
> Cisco

At Cisco, says Hoffman, the recognition of the importance of inclusive leaders is built into assessments and is part of next-generation leadership competencies. "Once we've built competencies, succession planning and rewards are built on those competencies," she says. The process of building competencies relies on role modeling; an important leadership component.

There has been a "seismic transformation" in Sodexo's culture since she joined the company 11 years ago, says Anand. "When I started there was diversity, but it was clustered at lower levels of the organization and it certainly was not the inclusive culture that we have today." Back then, she says, "folks did not necessarily feel they could bring their whole selves to work and be authentic in the workplace." Fast forward to 2013 and it's an entirely different situation. Today, she says: "We have a culture that is inclusive where people feel comfortable bringing their whole selves to work."

Gaining support from the top of the organization around inclusive leadership can also represent a barrier. While some savvy organizations—like Sodexo—embrace inclusive leadership at the top, not all do. "You can't assume that just because they're in the C-suite that they get it," says Quezada of Kraft. "You have to understand and you have to not only humble yourself, but you also have to learn to appreciate that they're on this journey as well and welcome them to participate in the journey."

In this environment, he says, business outcomes become a critical point of focus. "From a strategic focus, it gets back to outcomes. There's an emphasis and an enterprise perspective that are focused on outcomes. It's not only thinking of short-term results, but also thinking of long-term results now because you're thinking more broadly."

> It's not only thinking of short-term results, but also thinking of long-term results now because you're thinking more broadly.
> Jorge Quezada
> Kraft

A focus on gender and ethnicity, he says, has been a barrier that has led to missed opportunities.

"If you were just focused on gender and ethnicity five years ago, or if you're still there now, did you miss the generational challenges that are now in front of you? Are you missing out on how you're engaging your LGBT community at work? Do you have on your radar the whole disability perspective that, maybe, you should have? If you're just wired for gender and ethnicity, and your focus is on just those two things, you're going to miss these other dimensions of diversity in your conversations."

Inclusive leaders recognize that the focus needs to be much broader than that.

Identifying Outcome Measures

Inclusive leaders recognize that identifying outcome measures for their team and its performance, as well as for the organization as a whole, is critical to ensure success. How will you measure the impact of your inclusive behaviors? Through increased retention and reduced turnover? Through number of new ideas implemented? Through productivity gains? Through positive customer feedback? There are any numbers of ways that you can develop measures, establish baselines and monitor results.

It starts with a clear strategy, says Anand. Organizations need to clearly identify why they want to build a culture of inclusive leadership. Then they need to consider how they will know when they've been successful. At Sodexo, she says: "The attention is focused because we have a scorecard—people pay attention to what needs to happen because we're measuring their actions and behaviors. Accountability is critical.

"We continue to be a growth company. We continue to meet our growth targets. And I think a large part of that has to do with the culture that we have created primarily because it makes good business sense."

Accountability

At Sodexo, says Anand, the impacts of inclusive leadership are measured in multiple ways. One important barometer of the culture is an engagement survey that is conducted biannually. "At a time when the engagement scores for many companies have declined due to economic challenges, the overall engagement scores at Sodexo increased," she says. "This is quite a testament to the culture that we've created, but more importantly when we look at those engagement scores by race and gender, we find that minorities and women have some pretty significant increases that were driving the overall score."

Beyond engagement, Sodexo also has metrics tied to its scorecard that includes clear objectives. "People are held accountable through incentive compensation at a macro level and then through performance review at a micro, individual level," she says. Sodexo's scorecard has a heavy emphasis on behavioral metrics: "because you want to get the right behaviors to get to the right outcomes." This includes metrics related to leadership engagement, mentoring, sponsorship, training and developing high-potential talent. Measuring those things, she says, really gets to the "representation metrics" that companies have historically focused on.

That same approach is used at Cisco where, says Hoffman, inclusive leadership behaviors are built into assessments and rewards are based on how effectively leaders exhibit their ability to develop talent, drive succession planning and role model inclusive behaviors.

It's important for inclusive leaders to be able to demonstrate the value of their actions. Action and accountability are key! "Using tools that help identify leaders that exemplify inclusive leadership qualities, have better team member engagement, and better productivity will help quantify why these managers are generating more innovation, hence better results." The ability to measure the impact of inclusive leadership is "key," says Fernandez of FedEx Office. "When you have measurable components then you can take a look at those managers that are inclusive and really hone in on those competencies for the entire organization and, at the same time, you can look at the managers that are currently not displaying those behaviors and make it a point of emphasis for them so they can start to really do a better job in those core competencies."

> It's important for inclusive leaders to be able to demonstrate the value of their actions. Action and accountability are key!
>
> Manny Fernandez
> FedEx Office

Business Centered Framework

InclusionINC unveiled its Global InclusionSCORECARD™ at the 2013 Annual Conference Board Diversity & Inclusion Conference in New York City. The tool is designed to support the broad needs of organizations across many industries to offer a comprehensive path to make inclusion a core business strategy. Unlike traditional scorecards, the Global InclusionSCORECARD™ is part of an integrated and business-centered framework; it provides a consistent strategy for developing a culture of inclusion throughout the entire enterprise and aligning all leaders on key metrics, activities, behaviors and external stakeholder relations.

The focus needs to move beyond representation metrics to a fully comprehensive business centered framework. This framework must include

- monitoring and measuring inclusion results;

- rewarding and reinforcing inclusive leadership at all levels;

- integrating a culture of inclusion into values, principles and protocols;

- and creating an effective external strategy for growth markets and stakeholder relations.

By developing an integrated strategy around these leverage points, an organization is able to see an internal impact on productivity, innovation, engagement and retention and an external impact through selling more goods and services.

The use of scorecards tied to meaningful results that are aligned with business objectives is the foundation of inclusive leadership.

Out with the Old...

The old "command and control" approach to leadership is still hanging on, although there are signs that it may be diminishing. We are beginning to see more leaders moving beyond command and control and beginning to trust the insights and inputs of those one—or more—levels beneath them. In those that continue to practice old-style management, turnover and low productivity are prevalent. When people are not allowed to use their talent to contribute to their organizations they either "resign in place," or they leave. Neither is desirable. Ultimately, good employees will leave bad leaders to seek more inclusive, less command and control environments where they will be allowed to thrive.

Like it or not, trailblazers realize that inclusive leadership is the only way to keep an organization moving forward. Embracing inclusion is no longer something that can be relegated to the sidelines, or relegated to the HR department. Inclusion is not an HR initiative. Inclusion is a business imperative.

Key Takeaways

- While a "command and control" leadership style worked in an industrial society where productivity was measured in making widgets, today's knowledge-driven economy, that depends on harvesting innovative ideas, demands inclusive leadership.

- There are a number of CEOs who are now recognized as inclusive leaders; others can learn from their insights — and actions.

- Many organizations still lack the inclusive leadership traits and behaviors that will be required for them to succeed in the 21st century.

- Measurable business outcomes are the point of focus for determining the effectiveness of inclusive leaders.

- Inclusive leaders must hold themselves, and others, accountable for measurable outcomes tied to market demands.

- The Global InclusionsSCORECARD™ is a tool that can help organizations identify where they are currently and where they need to improve, to address internal and external pressures.

CHAPTER 8:
INCLUSIVE LEADER—THE BOTTOM LINE

There is a confluence of factors today impacting organizations and the leaders in them that requires changes in how they lead. These factors—an increasingly global economy, emerging markets, rapidly shifting demographics, the explosion of technology—require different ways of considering how work gets done. We no longer exist in an industrial economy where command and control can generate results internally and create products to sell to complacent customers. Today's leaders need a different profile—the profile of an inclusive leader. It is only through listening to the voices of internal and external individuals and leveraging the power of "thousands of eyes on the horizon" to enable organizations to thrive in a turbulent environment.

Driving the shift from traditional to inclusive cultures is not easy and it is not an effort that is ever "done." Even at companies as progressive as Sodexo, the impetus remains to be continually vigilant in developing inclusive leadership behaviors at all levels of the organization. "It's a continuum," says Anand, "and I don't think we will ever be done."

Even the most inclusive leaders will find that they still have people who will push back. They will have new employees coming on board. But, says Anand: "When you get a critical mass of people who are pushing in one direction, I think the naysayers have to get on board or they ultimately become irrelevant. You just need that critical mass of people who say, 'yes, this makes sense,' and they pull the others along."

Inclusive leaders must drive engagement internally and create connections externally by understanding and connecting to their markets and ensuring that their workforce is reflective of those markets—Key Employee Demographics Required for Growth.

Whether you're personally working to impact your team, or working to impact your organization, the inclusive traits of ego management, intellectual curiosity, being open to a wide range of inputs, transparency, emotional intelligence, futurecasting, humility, cultural agility, collaboration, accessibility, diversity of thought and adaptability are essential. You must develop or reinforce these traits and exhibit the associated behaviors that drive positive outcomes.

Self-Reflection and Feedback

A first step to becoming an inclusive leader is self-reflection which may involve seeking input from others about the extent to which you currently exhibit these traits. You may want to do a self-assessment and then ask others—friends, colleagues, team members, customers—to provide you with feedback as well. How does their perception of you mesh with your self-perception? Where are there opportunities for improvement?

Within your organization you might encourage other like-minded potential inclusive leaders to do the same. Together you could share feedback, discuss personal goals toward more inclusive leadership behaviors and form a community for support and collaboration.

Leaders Serving as Role Models

Inclusive leaders recognize, above all, that they must serve as role models to ensure that inclusive behaviors are spread across the organization.

"You need to be authentic yourself if you want those behaviors from others," says Anand. "Being transparent—being authentic—being someone that is role-modeling the behaviors that you want to see in your organization." At Sodexo, she says, a distributed leadership model helps to reinforce the desired culture across multiple locations at client sites. "For us, it's that distributed leadership model that helps to get the message out," she says. "We have a cross-market diversity council, we have our employee business resource groups, we have town halls. Every single message that we give has a diversity component to it. So, when the CEO goes out and does town halls, he also talks about diversity and inclusion."

Creating this culture can be challenging, especially for an

> We have a strategy and governance model that's top-down, bottom-up, and middle-out, where everyone is engaged in the success of transforming the organization.
> Rohini Anand
> Sodexo

organization as large and geographically dispersed as Sodexo. Globally, there are 420,000 employees in more than 35,000 locations. In the United States there are 125,000 employees in more than 10,000 locations.

"We have a strategy and governance model that's top-down, bottom-up, and middle-out, where everyone is engaged in the success of transforming the organization," says Anand. At Sodexo, and other organizations that have successfully embraced inclusive leadership, it's not just talk—inclusive leadership is monitored and measured to clearly identify business driven outcomes.

Carrying the Baton

Inclusive organizational leadership is an evolution, not a revolution. Depending on the culture within your organization, the path to inclusive leadership could be very short or excruciatingly long. Only you can decide whether it is worth it to fight the good fight where you are, or seek a leadership role in a more inclusive organization.

Sodexo has found itself in a unique position to influence other organizations. Most of Sodexo's managers operate out of client sites. "They go to work every day at the client sites," says Anand. "As our managers started understanding what we were doing and getting the tools and the communications, feeling the difference and realizing that we were transforming to a different organization, they started sharing with our clients.

"So we've not only impacted 125,000 employees in North America, but our clients' employees as well." Inclusive leaders can make a difference. Inclusive organizations can make a difference. Sodexo is a prime example. But they are not alone.

What are the best companies to work for in America today? In 2013, Fortune magazine took a look at its Fortune 500 list to see which companies on the list also showed up on its "best companies to work for list."

Their top picks were:

- Google
- NetApp
- Qualcomm
- Chesapeake Energy
- Devon Energy
- American Express
- Stryker
- Marriott International
- Darden Restaurants (Red Lobster, Olive Garden, The Capital Grille and LongHorn Steakhouse)
- Whole Foods[46]

What makes them so great? Things like an inclusive culture, work-life balance, training, good pay and benefits, and low turnover. Things like the opportunity for input and advancement, and the ability to make a difference. Of course, what makes any company "best" will be impacted by individual preferences

---

[46] Gordon, C. (2013, May 8). *Fortune 500: 10 Best Companies To Work For In 2013.* Retrieved from http://jobs.aol.com/articles/2013/05/08/fortune-500-best-companies-to-work-for-in-2013/#!slide=5870396

and personal values. The point is: inclusive leaders need to determine whether they want to work their magic from the top-down or the bottom-up. One path is short, the other often long.

What is immutable, however, in the current and future workforce is the value that the inclusive leader brings to the table. This new leadership model is creating significant business advantage <u>that will not soon become obsolete</u>.

Conclusion

While your organization may not be literally taken hostage by disgruntled employees as Specialty Medical Supplies' CEO was in 2013, it is highly likely for your organization to be figuratively hampered and taken hostage by outmoded thinking that threatens its ability to compete. An increasingly global economy, rapidly shifting demographics and an explosion of technology are impacting organizations seeking to succeed in this volatile business environment.

Inclusive leaders are poised to counter these threats. Their numbers are few but their path to improved performance guided by the identification of a number of traits that define success. As we move deeper into the 21st century it is clear that all leaders must become inclusive leaders.

CPSIA information can be obtained
at www.ICGtesting.com
Printed in the USA
LVOW10*0226170518

577522LV00005B/27/P